BANG THE STAGE,

Again!

A true-life account of an ordinary DJ

DAN MORRIS

Cover design by James Brinkler

Cover photo by Over the Moon Pictures
www.overthemoonpictures.co.uk

Published by Dan Morris
www.bangthestageagain.co.uk

ISBN: 979-8-8541782-4-2

"Don't think, just jock"

A phrase commonly used—or, if not, should be used—in situations when a person with a Dee-Jay skill often interferes with a lighting and sound engineer's area of expertise despite lacking the necessary knowledge.

For Nan (Joyce)

Contents

Chapter 1

Fire and Ice

It's a given fact that each of us has a dream in our lives. I'm not talking about standard dreams when you go to bed at night; I mean the dreams of ambition, a major goal to aim for in life. Some may have dreams of winning the lottery, owning a mansion with a swimming pool, being a professional football player, or being an astronaut when they grow up. I'm no different from anyone else. I had dreams as a young boy, ambitions, and life goals I wanted to achieve. They weren't to be an astronaut, a professional football player, or to have that mansion with a swimming pool. No, my ambitions were perhaps a little simpler. Mine was to be a firefighter, be a superstar top DJ, a radio presenter, and to one day complete Sonic the Hedgehog 3 on the Sega Mega Drive.

If you work hard at what you want, they say nothing is impossible and that if you dream it, you can do it. Another expression you hear is 'If you shoot for the stars and miss, you may land on the moon'. These are all very motivational quotes, and I like them to this very day, even though I've shot for the stars, completely missed the moon and ended up going through the rough end of a black hole many times. That said, out of my dreams, I did, I think, achieve them in one way or another. Make no mistake, it was no easy feat, and no matter how hard and frustrating things got at times, I knew I had to keep pushing forward. There were times I just wanted to throw in the towel and just give up, but every time I had that thought, I knew I'd come so far and couldn't give up. I had one gold ring left, and victory lay in one more turbo spin, and with that spin perfectly executed, I defeated Dr. Robotnik. I sat proudly on my Dennis the Menace-clad bed, put down the controller, and smiled as I unwrapped a red Opal fruit, watching on as Robotnik's spaceship blew up on my 15" Matsui tele. It was at that point that one of my life's dreams was ticked off. I was an 11-year-old boy when that achievement was completed in 1994. I was out of the traps with my dream-chasing and off to a good start. I just hoped my other dreams weren't going to be as hard to fulfil when the time came to try.

We always said to each other whilst setting up for a gig, "I wonder when our last gig will be." At the time, and unbeknownst to us, this was it.

South Shropshire, England.

South Shropshire is a beautiful county scattered with many little historic towns and villages, as well as having vast, open rolling hills and unspoilt countryside as far as the eye can see. It can also be very rural in some places. Growing up here as a young boy is a far cry from growing up in a busy town or city. Everything runs a little slower and sometimes a little behind the times in South Shropshire, but you're very lucky to have been brought up in such an unspoilt part of the world with a famous walking path, Offa's Dyke, that runs through there. Things you'd take for granted in a town or city would be an exciting event in South Shropshire. Take a weekend, for example. In a town or city, you'd be able to take a short walk from pub to pub and bar to bar before descending on your favourite nightclub. Not here. You could go to a pub, but you'd have two or maybe three at your disposal and at a walkable distance, and that's the end of the line unless you had a dedicated driver to then drive you at least 30 minutes to a town where you could find more pubs, bars and a nightclub. So when a dance, or 'Disco', was arranged in a local village hall or barn on a farm, this was an exciting event and one that would bring the hills and valleys to life at the weekend.

Now, if you will, compare this to Ibiza and the Balearics, the place where all superstar DJs go and play each summer, with blue skies, blue seas, bikinis, beach shorts, and sunsets. But who needs all that when you're a pair of young, enthusiastic budding DJs nearing the end of secondary school in Shropshire that have the hills, rain, dusty barns, a trusty Volvo 740 GL estate, a Land Rover Defender, a rusty Transit van with the bikinis and beach shorts swapped out for boiler suits, lewd polo shirts, wellies, and boots. This might not sound all that appealing and far less exciting in comparison with Ibiza, but believe me, you could create a great gig and a brilliant Saturday night out with the above ingredients. It was on the opposite side of the spectrum to town and city life on the weekend, with the bright lights of bars and nightclubs, but it was unique and different, and this is how it worked in rural Shropshire.

At weekends in Shropshire, the sleepy valleys came alive, thanks to the traditional pubs tucked away and an infamous group of young farmers in every village and town. The young farmers—or 'YFC' as they were known—were a collective group of, well, young farmers. Sons, daughters, brothers, sisters, and cousins of families that farmed Shropshire. In fact, you didn't have to be a farmer; anyone could join this infamous group. I admit, this sounds like the setting and the opening of some hammer horror story, but I can assure you it's not, and it's completely safe to read on. Simon Pegg and Nick Frost won't be rolling into Shropshire to save the day on this one.

The YFC had groups throughout Shropshire, like a youth club for teens and young adults, if you like. In pretty much every village in Shropshire, you'll find a YFC club. They all got involved in different events and social gatherings throughout the year, which included a good dance to let off some steam at the weekend! These dances they held were all over the county, some big, some small, some in marquees and some in barns, anywhere really that they could fit in a few hundred people. All they needed was a venue, some imagination, a bar with copious amounts of beer and cider, and of course a DJ. And this is where we come in, and this is where we start our journey of the times of our lives and my attempt at becoming that superstar DJ.

'DJ's Fire and Ice... The Beginning'—that was the official title of our first official mix tape as an unstoppable DJ duo, and it was an absolute banger of a tape. Boy, the name itself would stop you in your tracks whilst digging through the new releases in a record shop, wouldn't it? No, it really wouldn't, but try telling that to a couple of 15-year-old

DJs that had a set of budget vinyl decks set up in the loft of his mum and dad's bungalow with a handful of records fresh from the local pub's jukebox. In reality, though, off stage and out of the loft, my name was Dan, and my sidekick was Andy—or Lewis, as we called him. He was very inventive, as this was his surname.

We were sort of two ordinary teenage boys growing up in a little Shropshire village called Newcastle on Clun. I should say Lewis was growing up in Newcastle, and I was two miles down the road in a tiny little hamlet nestled between the village of Clun and Newcastle on Clun called Whitcott Keysett. It was a blink and you'll miss it kind of place if you drove through it, but I was always found in Newcastle with Lewis and a whole bunch of other great lads, on our bikes, having a kick around at the local playing fields, fishing, shooting, setting up a tent ready to camp the weekend away, and keeping a look out whilst Lewis was sneaking out of his dad's garage with a coffee jar full of petrol to get the campfire lit. When not found doing those activities, the chances are you'd find us both up in the loft at his mum and dad's bungalow in our 'makeshift' DJ/lads space studio that we'd constructed with some ply boards on the roofing trusses, which separated us from the Christmas decorations and the usual items that are stored in a loft.

This was, I guess, the closest you could get to having your own one-bed apartment whilst still living at home, minus the kitchen and bathroom, but that was directly below us on the ground floor, and it was just a matter of squeezing through the smallest gap ever out of the studio, smashing your head on a beam, and climbing down the loft latch with a mild concussion and sometimes a nail in your head to use the facilities and the first aid kit as and when required.

We loved our little studio; it was a work of art, and we were very proud of it. In our studio, we had a window, an armchair, a dart board, a TV complete with VCR and cassette player, a table we had out of a skip set up with our DJ decks on, a psychedelic thick pile rug, a few/several FHM lady posters, breeze block walls, a Commodore c64, some copper pipes, and a water tank. What else could a young pair of budding teenage DJs want? We loved it that much that on each New Year's Eve, we'd spend the entire night up there, with a couple of cheeky cans of Skol lager, listening to the likes of Judge Jules or Dave Pearce live on BBC Radio 1 doing DJ sets, thinking that one day that could be us.

We had visions and dreams of making it to the top; now we had all the gear. We even stamped the date of the first mix tape we did in history. Well, we marked it up on the scoreboard of the Winmau dartboard we had in the loft, and to this very year, it is still marked up on that dartboard, although that dart board has now since moved with Lewis to his own house as it would be a bit weird if he still spent all his time being a grown man with a young family shut off in the loft of the bungalow, but if he did choose to do that, I'd still be his mate.

Fire and Ice, we labelled ourselves. Where we got our inventive titles from, I have no idea. We didn't even really know who was DJ Fire and who was DJ Ice? Something we could have easily sorted, though, should Top of the Pops come calling one day. I think I would have been DJ Fire owing to my red hair, and Lewis would have been Ice—as in cool as ice, as he did have the most perfect, summer of 97' catalogue style, symmetrical set of curtains as a haircut I'd ever seen and was quite envious of. It was an immaculate cut and so neat and strong because of all the hairspray and gel that went on it. I think most '90s haircuts were strong and flammable. I did attempt to adopt the same cool cut as every teenage lad did in the 1990s, however, mine looked more like wet loft insulation. Still, I tried.

The whole DJ thing came at a very young age, for me, at least. I knew I was put on this planet to DJ when I remixed Jeff Wayne's 1978 musical, The War of the Worlds, in 1991; I was about eight years old. I didn't technically remix it; what I actually did was put it on Mum and Dad's vinyl deck player and scratched the seven shades of s**t out of it, quite literally, like a DMC world champ. Once I'd finished scratching with that and had enough of my version of a 19th-century Martian invasion gone wrong, I'd move on to Dad's favourite: Rod Steward LP. I'd get through as many of their vinyls as possible until the needle broke or I burnt the motor out, really. They used to get quite cross with me; my sister's budgie and Sammy loved my performances though, he'd be on his perch bobbing up and down like a good un' before battering his cuttlefish.

Lewis, on the other hand, had always been big into his music. When I first met him at the local youth club in around 1995, we hit it off straight away with our love for the same music, and we always sat next to each other on the school bus, sharing an earphone and listening to mix tapes. Our folks were smart and could see the potential we both had to be big hitters, so they organised a DJ to come along to the local youth club one Friday night. It was that night, after Lewis and I clapped eyes on proper DJ decks, that we were bitten by the bug. It wasn't long before a big box turned up on his doorstep which was all we needed to get on the road as DJs.

So, armed with a pair of budget belt-driven vinyl turntables, a jukebox cast off vinyl, an amplifier, a pair of bookshelf speakers, and a top-of-the-range studio to perfect our skills in, we were ready to headline Creamfields—almost, just a gig would be a good start.

On most weekends, Lewis and I would go out and study the dances that were held by the YFC at the Newcastle Village Hall in aim of getting some idea of how they went and what the DJ would play. Obviously, at that time, we weren't old enough to get into one of these dances at the village hall, so what we actually did was perch ourselves in some hedgerow next to the village hall and observe from there the people going in and out and get close enough to hear what music the DJ was playing. If a rogue pint was accidentally left outside by anyone having a chat, we may have sprung out and cleared it away at times in the cover of darkness, like a couple of Wombles in the hedgerow. Once our position in the hedgerow was compromised, we took to a new position that was slightly further away but still close enough to keep an eye on things. We located ourselves near a couple of huge logs that were in the primary school's playground. This was a completely new world for us and one that, when we were old enough, we'd want a slice of. I think our direction in life could have taken a turn here. We would either continue with our DJing journey, start working in some form of the intelligence sector, or be arrested.

Now, whilst we waited for the gigs to come our way, and with daybreak, Lewis and I were savvy and got involved with the local production work down at that same village hall. It was a lovely new building for the village and had been built the previous year, replacing the old, dilapidated village hall in the summer of 1996. By getting involved with the local production work, it meant that for any amateur dramatics, bands, plays, etc. that the village hall was booked for, we would be the main stage, sound, and lighting engineers for the job, which basically meant that we would grab a rickety pair of stepladders out of the store room and move a few dusty lights into position for the main event. However, the village hall did have something that caught our attention, partially hidden behind the mops and the cleaning products: a pair of Peavey speakers far superior to our bookshelf ones in our studio; they also had a nice mixer too, which we thought would be perfect for accommodating our first headlining gig when the call came in. So, we continued to offer our technical services and enthusiasm to the village hall for productions, hoping that when the call came, the village hall committee, in turn, would kindly lend us the speakers and mixer to rock Wembley Arena. Smart move.

Lewis and I continued to spend all our time shut off from the world in a roof space until word of mouth got around that we were the new big thing. We had no social media back then, so word of mouth was all we had. We didn't know if we would actually ever get a gig, to be honest with you, but one day the strangest thing happened: someone got desperate, and we got a gig. It was time to take the show out of the loft and on the road and show the world, or Newcastle Village Hall, what we were made of. Hold tight.

Chapter 2
The Call

Fully established in 1997, and word of mouth spreading quicker than our petrol-drenched campfires about the hottest new musical talent in the Clun Valley, the call finally came in. It was a private birthday party booked at the Newcastle Village Hall, where we assisted; it wasn't a call to support The Chemical Brothers; nonetheless, it was a gig we had to prepare for. We were out of the traps like a couple of greyhounds, and luckily, our plan of borrowing the village hall speakers came into play, and they kindly said we could use them, so that was one little issue instantly taken care of. One thing that was a big issue, as we quickly realised, was our vinyl collection. This was something to be desired, you see. We had no choice in what we got when we were given the innards of the pub jukebox when the landlord had the music changed around, but beggars certainly couldn't be choosers in our current position, and we took whatever we were given with gratitude; it was almost like a lucky dip, and we had no idea what we had until we got back to the studio to see. It soon came to light that we had no current chart music, just trance and dance music that we personally liked at the time, and the best we could dig out of our vinyl cast-offs was 'Satan' by Orbital and 'Block Rockin' Beats' by The Chemical Brothers. All the latest chart music, which we desperately needed, was left behind in the jukebox.

Surprisingly, we both had enough sense and had hung about in enough hedgerows and logs now to realise that the vinyl we had wouldn't be sufficient for our debut gig and wouldn't get the party started, let alone finish it. Years previously, I think our common sense about music had been thrust into us by the local DJ at the time, John, or 'DJ Long John', as he was known. John was a lovely chap and a very good party DJ. He used to DJ at our youth club parties back when Lewis and I were a lot younger, at the old Newcastle village hall. We would go there at seven on a Friday night; you'd have a pound in your pocket, which would get you a refresher sweet and a cup of warm, flat coke served up in a beat-up tin beaker that looked like it had been forged from scrap. Then, with a big sugar rush on board and confidence peaking, you'd take to the dance floor, dancing like there's no tomorrow before ending your mad moment by skidding down the hall on your knees, burning the knees out on your best tracksuit, whilst your mum looked on in disgust at you showing off like a complete tit. That's what a Friday night was all about: holes in your tracksuit, carpet-burnt knees, and enough built-up static in your body that the only natural way to discharge it was to run over to your sister as quick as you could and touch her ear. Good times.

Anyway, I digress. Being a birthday party, you'd have a vast age range of people there. Whilst a few of the 'younger' ones may have liked a select few tracks we had on vinyl, Lewis and I couldn't really imagine Joyce, Dot, and Edith throwing their glow sticks in the air whilst wearing a bucket hat and blowing fiercely on a whistle as we played music from The Chemical Brothers and Orbital. However, that would have been extremely entertaining. So, with that little musical predicament standing in our way, we dug deep into our pockets, expressed the urgency of preparation to Lewis's mum, and she drove us over to the local Woolworths shop, a 30-minute drive over the border into Wales to Newtown, Powys, where we splashed the little cash we had on every new CD single we could possibly afford! It didn't matter at that time whether we liked it or not; as long as it was popular with the public and had a little bit of something for all ages and was enough to get them onto the dance floor, then we were winning. A few years later, one smart man told me that "every track is someone's favourite track," which was a very good thing to always remember.

We had the basics in place to be a successful duo; it may not have been a trance music gig that we were both into, but it was a start. Yes, we had to sacrifice the Gatecrasher albums and our street cred for 'C'est La Vie' by B*Witched and 'Dancing Queen' by ABBA. But did that matter? Not to us, it didn't; we were going to be proper DJs, and to be honest, it was going to be a nice change to play to a live dance floor in the village hall instead of to a poster of Jordan and Caprice in the loft, blu-tacked onto some ply board in front of us. We had and were suffering a few minor teething problems starting out. You may well have noticed that I've been talking about vinyl a lot, and that's all we had: vinyl turntables and limited vinyl to play. But things took a turn when we got this debut gig. We needed CDs, and CDs were the thing; we just didn't have a CD player. That was the next issue we had to get around, but luckily for us, Lewis had a younger sister, Ellie, who did have a CD player. Ellie was kindly going to lend us this single CD-loading player for our gig; she just didn't know it yet.

The thing is, when you're in your mid-teens and you have a younger sister, it's a given that you don't share with your siblings, and getting that CD player out of her bedroom with her permission and to the village hall wasn't going to be the smoothest of operations. Unfortunately, I can't remember exactly how we managed to get possession of it, and I dread to think of the amount of hardship it was. Lewis had probably had to have handed over all of his crisps Walkers Tazos he was collecting at the time or something similar, but the important thing was we did, and now, with some turntables and an obscure selection of vinyl records, a CD player, a pair of village hall speakers, and the entire top 40 of that week that financially crippled us from Woolworths in our collection, we were ready to raise the roof. There was just one more thing missing— some disco lights.

This wasn't to be a problem, though, which makes a nice change. We could have tried to hook up the stage lighting in the village hall we maintained, although, between us, we wouldn't have had a clue how to get them programmed to flash like they do at concerts. We would need a real technical genius to sort that out for us; we did get a tech wizard on board, but he comes later. For now, it was a quick bike ride round to our mates Jonny and Anthony, aka 'The Twins'—two twin brothers who also lived in the village and whom we spent lots of our free time with, to borrow a super awesome, jaw-dropping set of four flashing bulbs that were music-sensitive that were enclosed in a box. Do you know the ones? They were novelty disco party lights that had a red, yellow, blue, and green bulb that was enclosed in a little rectangular metal box.

It wasn't Glastonbury main stage standards, but if you drew all the curtains in the village hall, switched off all the lights, and just waited long enough until it got dark outside, you'd get at least a square metre of colour to dance in as the end result. With that all said, and all implications overcome and ironed out, we were primed and ready to go! And we did; I won't bore you all and go into describing every single minute of each gig I describe, and this gig, even though it was officially our first gig, I can't really remember much about it, which is sad, and I wish I could, but from what I remember, it was a success! We did it! We did our first official gig! Local heroes.

One thing I did forget to mention, though, was that prior to the gig, we liaised with our agents and decided to drop the 'Fire and Ice' title. It was a little too heavy and childish, we decided, so we simply went with the more imaginative title of 'DJs Dan and Andy' much more grown-up and fitting. That was until someone had too many Worthington Creamflows on board one evening and thought it clever and inventive to combine both our names and come up with the name 'Dandy' as we appreciated their input and concern over our stage name, we decided to stay with the original title and thanked them all the same, and probably got them another pint of Worthy.

So, with one gig firmly under our belts, we took our earnings of £30, walked out of the village hall and into the sunset of the Clun valley, and were left wandering when and where our next DJ gig would be. It wasn't long before it presented itself.

Chapter 3
The Wheels (of steel) In Motion

Another gig came in off the success of our debut, and this time it was in the form of my mum's 40th. We were now in 1998, Mum wanted a party for the big one, and luckily for her, she now had a pair of professional DJs at her disposal. It was the summer of June. Mum had booked the Newcastle village hall for her party, which was good as we were well established there as it's the same venue we played our debut gig, plus once we had shifted the mops, polish, and a great big industrial floor cleaner thing that had a great big abrasive disc on, it gave us easy access to the village halls speakers and mixer again.

Payment negotiations were tough on this, though. We were charging £30 per gig. Can you charge your own family the full going rate? I wanted to and really needed to, however, I understood it was big money, so I settled for a few lifts on a Friday night to the local pub to play pool and enough brass in my pocket to get myself a pint of shandy and Kylie's latest single for the next gig. I'm not too sure what Lewis did with his cut. Most likely threw it back into the pot to buy another random CD he didn't want to be seen with in his collection.

Now, at this point, things were looking a little more hopeful and hassle-free. I had a Kenwood three-disc changing Hi-Fi sitting proudly in my bedroom at home—a Kenwood XD-751, to be precise. I think it was a Christmas present one year. I can't really remember, and it doesn't matter anyway. This shiny lump of silver, with its three-disc changing capability, two-deck cassette, and a display that did all that posh, flashy stuff, was a thing of beauty. It also came in very handy and would save the hassle of having to borrow Lewis' sister's CD player again for future gigs; we used the Kenwood instead, which I think made Lewis very happy as it would save him from owing future big debts to his sister.

By this time, we had permanently ditched the vinyl

turntables and left them gathering dust in the loft because we discovered the collection of vinyl we had and continued to receive just wasn't getting any better and wasn't suitable for the clientele we were entertaining at this point in our DJ career.

We continued to blow more money than we had coming in on all the CDs from Woolworths in Newtown, and I was taking huge risks by now and having to ask, beg, borrow, and, well, steal my younger sister Jess's BoyZone, Savage Garden, and Spice Girls albums, amongst others. So I was now also in shark-infested water, the same as Lewis, with an ongoing younger sister war. Getting a gig was great, but we had to crawl over broken glass to get the music to do it. Lewis and I were both men down with this battle each time we secured a gig, Lewis had mounting debt every time he approached his sister's bedroom door, and I had to cross a minefield and try to dodge Jackie Chan standing on the other side of the door.

With the 'sister' dilemma becoming a struggle, we decided to cut our losses and went at it alone with Kenwood, which worked to a fashion. Playing a CD and watching people dance to the track playing was great, as you'd expect, having to play another track off another CD once that track had finished...well, that was interesting. After the one track had finished playing, you had to press the two or three button to change the disc, so with a dance floor full of people, they had to take a 30-second breather whilst the next CD and track loaded up. They had time to go to the bar and get a drink if the CD that got changed was scratched and automatically changed again! Watching that next CD load up eagle-eyed, hoping it would successfully load and play, felt like the same amount of pressure as when a major football match went to penalties. To put it into context, imagine watching a gripping programme on TV, then every four minutes, there was an ad break; that was what it was like. That said, this was only our second 'real' gig, and these were all minor teething issues and learning curves, which you'd expect. Everyone seemed to enjoy the night, including my mum, who's birthday it was and didn't mind too much about the little break they had between disc changes, as it gave more people to time to catch up on things. Lewis and I performed the best we could that night with what we had, and we got another successful(ish) gig under our belts and onto our CV, even if it did feel about as smooth as driving a car with no clutch.

In 1998, although we were using our initiative and using a bedroom Hi-Fi to DJ with, CD DJing was actually a genuine and relatively new thing. It was evolving in the professional world, slowly becoming a popular addition used by top DJs alongside their vinyl decks. But these purpose-built professional CD Players or, or CDJs as they are called, were mega bucks, far too expensive for a couple of total amateurs like us on £30 a gig, so until we had the confidence to charge £1000 a night and be booked five nights a week by a client that was happy to pay this fee, we had to do the best we could with what we got and adapt and overcome the CD changing pause.

And adapt and overcome we did! We had no choice. After some time, a very long time standing by the phone waiting for the next gig to be booked, the phone one day rang, and just like that, we got booked for another gig, but not just any other gig. We just got booked for the ultimate gig—the ultimate gig for many DJs worldwide, for that matter. I've no idea to this day how it came about, and it really doesn't matter because we were fed up with standing by the phone, but we secured this gig, which was a huge step up for us, and it presented absolutely no pressure for us whatsoever.

Chapter 4
Millennia

We're now in 1999; Lewis and I have been an ensemble for two years and racked up a staggering two gigs on our tour of the valley, even though the previous two gigs were at the same venue. So, we were doing well, apart from a long wait between gigs.

Life as two teenage superstar DJs from Shropshire breaking the big time was tough, as we were finding out, but it became harder and even more comical to friends due to the release of the Kevin & Perry Go Large movie. It was a brilliant film, and we loved it and related to it so much, and the soundtrack to it was immense. But it didn't do us any favours, not one single bit, because Harry Enfield's character, Kevin, was ginger-haired for a start - It wasn't a problem, as I considered myself to be more Moroccan sunset shade of non-ginger anyway, but it was kind of cool, really, that he was a 'ginger' DJ; the stars were aligning, I thought; the problem then came when they were stamped with the infamous nicknames that I need not repeat. I remember watching the film at the cinema when it came out, and as soon as their nicknames came out, that's when, for a second, I thought that could be an issue. Anyway, we pushed forward in these tough times and focused all our attention on this big gig, even if we got stamped with the same nickname as Kevin & Perry did in the film for the next few months, which never got boring.

What's this ultimate gig, then? Well, 'DJs Dan and Andy' got the 1999 into 2000 millennium Young Farmer's gig, no less. Let me tell you, this was a huge step up for us, as you can probably imagine, with our extensive back catalogue of two gigs so far, and we knew that this was a foot in the door for many more gigs to come flowing, hopefully.

This was a big deal. It was being held in a bigger village hall than we were normally used to playing in, which wasn't hard as we had only played in one village hall previously. This was being held in the Clun Memorial Hall within the grounds of some playing fields in the neighbouring village of Clun, four miles down the road from Newcastle on Clun. It was a fantastic village hall and venue to play; as you entered the hall through some glass doors, you would be met in a foyer and be greeted by door staff who'd be sat with a fold-up table, a tin money box, and some wristbands. Once you'd passed this point, you'd enter a corridor with those big, cooker-ring-type heaters that would very nearly set fire to your head. You had to run past those if you were wearing too much nylon or polyester. If you got past those successfully without your Joop cologne and shirt combusting or even getting shrink-wrapped, you'd then open a set of double doors that opened up into the hall itself facing the stage, complete with a bar to your left that ran by the local pub, which was surrounded by a nice sticky floral carpet.

The stage was a great one to play on, too. It was far wider and deeper than Newcastle village hall, which meant plenty more room to fill with lighting. Just off to the side of the stage, there were a few little steps that you went down, which led to a little toilet and dressing room, which was really convenient. Anyway, back to the gig. Playing in the Clun Memorial Hall, meant that we had a bigger venue to play in, a bigger stage to fill, which we had absolutely no idea how to do, 400 people to entertain, and the biggest party of the millennium to play, and all we had was a Kenwood triple-changing Hi-Fi in our arsenal and a set of four flashing bulbs. It was at this point that we well and truly came to realise that we were in over our heads and were left wandering why we had accepted this gig.

Keeping 400 party people waiting 30 seconds whilst a CD changed on the biggest night of the millennium just wouldn't be good for a start, so we reluctantly and with no other option, went back to Lewis' sister, cap in hand, ready to rack up more debt in exchange for her CD player again to add to the setup. I nervously and bravely walked the plank to my sister's bedroom door, prepared to do battle for the boyband albums, although if we survived the battle, at least this way we could play one track after the next without a gap, and we had the usual big hit CDs at the time, so there was good reason to battle on, but this was just the tip of the iceberg. After getting the CDs and the CD player, we had a long, long way to go yet in order to pull off a successful night of entertainment.

We were seriously underpowered with speakers; even borrowing the Newcastle Village Hall speakers wasn't going to be enough, and those flashing box lights struggled in a small village hall, so in the Clun Memorial Hall, they would have given off the effect of a lit match. What in the name of all that's holy were we going to do here? There were three things that we needed: never to have agreed to do the gig for one, pray for a miracle, or for my mum to buy a mobile disco.

Chapter 5
Mum Bought a Mobile Disco

In the classified advertisements in the newspaper, as luck would have it, mum read that someone was retiring from the mobile disco business and had listed a complete set-up for sale at a reasonable price. Instead of ignoring that, she did a kind thing and thought it might suit us. A call was made, and a meet-up with this seller was organised. I remember borrowing the Newcastle village hall for a few hours whilst this man and his van turned up and spilled the contents of his equipment over the floor. Looking back now, it was very basic, dated equipment, but we didn't care! It was certainly an upgrade from what we had. It was 1999, and this equipment was from the late 80s, but it was equipment, and it's what we needed, minus the odd bit here and there.

I still remember how puzzled I was to find a set of fairground lights in the package. You know, the strip lights that had a row of coloured bulbs you'd see down the metal arms of a ride at a fun fair? Yes, those. We had a pair of them for some reason. There was also a pair of all-in-one vinyl turntables, which I think were last used in the Spit & Sawdust saloon in the wild west and had a date of 1867 on them. They were older than god's dog and were unfortunately shelved from the start.

But two things, hidden in two small flight cases, made our faces light up. There were two CD players! We forgot the rest for a moment; it was marvellous. We had two CD players, and Lewis could now rest easy and relax some.

After rifling through all the equipment, I remember my mum asking me if I was serious about this and really wanted to do it, just like when you're young in a shoe shop trying on some new shoes for school, like, do they fit? Go for a walk around the shop? Check where your toe pops up at the end of the shoe, etc. She went through that routine. Of course, I agreed and said yes a million times. Well, the mobile set-up never went back in that man's van, and 'DJs

Dan and Andy' were now the proud new owners of a full Butlins retro disco, which had probably entertained many back in the summer of '86 and got packed up in the back of Mum's Volvo and unloaded into Mum and Dad's spare living room, which eventually became the equipment stock room much to their delight.

All that was missing that didn't come with it all was a couple of yellow blazers that would have made us look smart as carrots standing behind that setup. We were very grateful to her for helping us like that, and it definitely put us up the ladder a few steps, even if it was a rickety wooden one with woodworm. Now, during this year, 1999, and several months before the millennium gig, there was a man; he delivered car parts to my dad. My dad was a self-employed mechanic, who owned his own little successful business out of a workshop in Whitcott Keysett, South Shropshire. This man, Dave Cornish, delivered car parts as a side job to mechanics and garages in and around the area whilst he built up another part of his own business. His main business was called Red Flame Productions, which was a sound and lighting hire business; he also did mobile gigs and events, just like we were starting, or, should I say, attempting to start! Dave was also a certified professional DJ and held a residency at Crystals nightclub, which was in his local town of Newtown in Mid Wales, the same town where we held a residency at Woolworths.

With regular weekly deliveries from Dave to my dad, word got out that I was a young budding DJ and was venturing into this industry. Dave was asked if he had any help or advice he could give me, and he did. He had plenty of invaluable help and advice, but not only that; he also had some work experience. He gave me the opportunity to go along with him to some of his gigs and get involved with how it all gets put together. I spent a lot of time with Dave at weekends on the road, assisting as a 'roadie' with gigs he did, and I absolutely loved it! From loading the vans up with some other great lads to setting up, this was all an essential experience. Watching him DJ was incredible, as it was the first live DJ I could watch that could professionally beat mix on a pair of vinyl turntables. It was fascinating to me. I remember the amount of DJ equipment he had—a vast amount of very expensive, high-end equipment that I could only ever dream of having myself one day—all housed in a huge underground warehouse-type room underneath the nightclub. Although I was disappointed to find out he never had any fairground lights like we did, I did offer them to him in conversation one day, but he was too kind a man to accept this gift and politely declined my offer.

I spent many a weekend getting driven over to Newtown in the front of the Volvo estate by mum, I think she used to be glad to get rid of me at the weekends, to be honest, as it was quieter around the house with no music rattling the rafters and her not having to think about calling in a structural engineer, although she did have to endure Pete Tongs Essential Selection for the 40-minute drive at quite some volume.

Mind you, I didn't get off lightly, and I did get a taste of my own medicine, especially when I got into Dave's Range Rover to head to a gig. Dave was a pro DJ, and I'm adamant it has taken its toll on his hearing. I remember he used to put a Clubbers Guide to Ibiza CD on, and he had a bass cannon in the boot right behind my head. This meticulously rearranged my insides many a time and practically rendered me deaf for the evening, so much so that after Dave's Range Rover concert, followed by the gig we were heading to, when mum picked me up on Sunday morning, I was quite happy to listen to her UB40 tape on much-reduced volume on the journey home after she had stopped off to do the weekly food shop at Kwik-Save.

Right, let's get back on track...

We had some time to prep for this millennium gig. We'd test-driven the kit we now had and had a plan in mind. There were, however, a couple of items missing, a fog machine and a strobe light. These were must-have items, but this wasn't a problem. A quick phone call to my mate, Dave, and luckily, these items were secured for our gig.

As Dave was booked with numerous gigs each weekend and more so on New Year's Eve, we had to make do with whatever he had spare on shelves of his warehouse, and with that, two broken, beat-up plastic boxes turned up, and within them was a strobe light that was borderline legal and would never pass health and safety legislation today due to being 50x brighter than a bolt of lightning, and would also leave you holding your breath when you pushed the button, hoping it didn't trip the fuse box of the venue. Then there was the fog machine that was rusty, dented, leaked everywhere, and produced super thick, dense smoke that could set a fire alarm off within a two-mile radius. I often wondered if, after a blast of fog, we would still have a full dance floor of people dancing or would they all be unconscious, overcome by its rough emissions? Thankfully, they were always still upright, but no doubt they all had tight chests and wheezed a bit.

If you have a little bit of OCD and like things to look neat and tidy, this setup wouldn't have been for you, and to be honest, when we think back to how it looked, it makes us cringe too. Our minds were too focused on the end result to worry about what colour our cables were or how they were all assembled. I mean, we had cables everywhere; it was an absolute mess. We had reels and reels of extension leads strewn everywhere—white ones, and I remember a big, thick industrial orange one too. All the cables were hanging freely from the lighting stand, which was basically two or three curtain poles that were fastened together with masking tape, rested on top of the speakers at each end, and taped down. Once that was up, we hung the lights from it using insulation tape.

Thinking back, how we managed to defeat gravity and not pull all that down is beyond me. It was absolute trickery. The whole set-up was as fragile as a game of Jenga and looked like the aftermath of a fire in an office block when the false ceilings collapsed with all the cables hanging down. Make no mistake, it was that bad, but we didn't care. Once the lights were all switched off and ours came on, no one would see it anyway. Thankfully, in later years, we did turn our attention more to aesthetics and tidied up our act. If anything, we probably got OCD too in the end. Our rigs were that tidy and neat; they looked like permanent fixtures, and it was a shame to pack them down at the end of a gig. I'm happy to report that we also invested in some proper lighting stands, and masking tape and curtain poles were never used again.

So, New Year's Eve arrived, and we were all set up with lighting bars taped together with masking tape, lighting hung with insulation tape, 2x CD players, that week's top 40 on CD, a fog machine that kept the local fire station on edge, and a lethal strobe light that would X-ray you. We may have been a health and safety reps' nightmare and void from any form of public liability insurance, but we were ready to throw the biggest party of our two-year, two-gig career, and nothing was going to stop us.

Chapter 6
Hot Stuff

At 8:00 p.m. sharp, the doors to the hall were opened, and we were up and running with some background music. The bar served drinks, and the good people were coming in thick and fast, filling up the all-important dance floor. In no time, that was packed, so we ramped up the music and kicked off the night, and nobody noticed or commented on our scrap heap show on the stage. Nice.

Things were going smoothly for us, but now we were just about to hit a problem.

We underestimated the amount of audio power we needed to keep the music loud. It was okay to start, but as the village hall filled, we started to get underpowered by the volume, which is a horrible feeling. You just seem to instantly lose the atmosphere when that happens. We pushed the volume up on the amps as far as they'd gotten before they distorted, and the mixer was about ready to show us its red lines, but thankfully this was just enough to keep the vibe going. Just! We were already thinking about how we were going to replace the village hall speakers we borrowed from the other village hall after we had to tell them we'd blown them. Lewis wouldn't have been any help with finances, as he was already snowed under with debt to his sister. Poor lad.

Then, with already 10 bags of nerves and stress, our second problem presented itself: one of the amps was running incredibly hot. I mean, it was that hot, you could have cooked breakfast on it! Seriously hot! I knew nothing about amplifiers, but with anything running this hot, I knew this wasn't good. This sent Lewis and me into a right spin now. What happens now if the amp packs in and kills all the music? What a disaster this would be! And all before the biggest countdown to a new year ever!

We had to think fast; in an instant, an idea sprung into my head. With that, I propelled myself off the stage like an Olympian and ran to the kitchen, where I spotted a desk fan earlier. I grabbed it and ran back as quickly as I could to get it plugged in and onto the amp to cool it down before we had a mass silence followed by a mass riot on our hands!

They always say things come in threes, and bang on cue, here entered problem number three. You might ask yourself how hard it could be to plug in a fan. Not that hard at all if you have a free plug. However, we didn't. What we did have was more wires than a telephone exchange on the stage, and every extension lead had a plug in it, unlabelled. We had to try and work out which plug could be spared. There was one that a desk lamp was plugged into, but when you've got a million cables thrown on top of everything, a dark hot stage, pressure on you, and trying to actually DJ at the same time, working out which plug to pull without losing sound or lighting was like trying to work out whether to cut the red wire or blue wire on a bomb you see in the films.

I was on my knees, squashed under a table; time was ticking, and my heart rate was increasing quite significantly. Done, I pulled a plug. I turned my head to the side, the sound was still on. Success, I thought, but when I heard a rowdy crowd and scrambled backward from under the table and stood up feeling relieved, I soon realised that the plug I pulled had plunged the dance floor into total darkness, either that or the millennium bug had bitten earlier than anticipated. The only light that was left on was the pathetic little desk lamp still casting light over the CDs. Back under the table, I went like a rabbit down a hole to resolve the minor issue. I hated that lamp from then on. After what felt like an hour, the lighting was back on, and cold air from the fan was cooling the amplifier down. Thank God, we were back on track to 'hopefully' see the biggest new year we will see. I think at this point, though, myself and Lewis, despite having this huge step up doing this gig, would have much rather been back in the attic with Jordan and Caprice, a tin of Skol lager in hand, whilst listening to the Judge on BBC Radio 1 doing it properly.

Chapter 7
Hello and Goodbye

Lewis and I were rocking the dance floor at long last at this 1999 – 2000 gig. Everything was actually working as it should, and people hadn't left, which was a pleasant surprise. Just as we thought it was safe to breathe again and start relaxing a little, this figure of a man, through the dense smoke, approached the stage and heaved himself upon it.

"Hey, mate," I heard him say, "any chance I could request a song, please?"

"Yes, sure, not a problem." (No idea what the song was.) "I'll get it on as soon as I can for you, I replied. "Cheers, mate." When people jumped up onto the stage to request songs, they would normally ask, then jump back down and carry on with their night. This lad, though, hung around for a minute, interested in what was going on and taking it all in. Before he jumped back down off the stage, he came back over to me and asked, "Why have you got that fan on the amp?" I explained the problem we had earlier, and he laughed. "You've got the fan on the heat sync," he said. "What's that?" I replied cluelessly. "The bit that's designed to take the heat out of the amp to stop it overheating," he said, still laughing. I looked at Lewis and then turned back and said, "So I don't need the fan on the amp, then?" "No," he said. What an absolute pair of prats. I felt like a right plank! All that stress for absolutely no reason at all! That bloody amp was meant to be hot. It was doing its job. It was at this point that I firmly realised that I was good with music knowledge, but for the technical side, I was absolutely useless and, at that particular moment, felt about as much use as a wet newspaper.

"Well, mate, I feel a little more relaxed now. Thanks for that. Oh...I'll play your track next," I said.

"Cheers, mate," he replied and jumped back down to dance.

A little later, he came back up and asked for another track, and he hung around a little longer this time. I didn't mind him hanging around, as he wasn't being a pest or getting in the way. He was just curious and interested in what Lewis and I were doing. We chatted between tracks, and towards the end of the night, he asked us if he could come with us on a gig in the future, to which I said yes pretty much instantly, given his immense knowledge of desk fans and amplifiers. I saw the potential in that young man right away.

Lewis asked, "Who's he? Do you know him?" "That's Mark Richardson; I went to school with him. Nice lad. Not spoken to him for years," I replied.

Well, we did it. With plenty of Sash, Steps, and the Vengaboys played, no tripped fuse boxes, an education into why amps get hot, and no one suffering from smoke inhalation, we dragged our way through New Year's Eve 1999 into 2000 and faced a new millennium, and our third and possibly final gig was wrapped. Unfortunately, it was to be our third and final gig, as DJs Fire and Ice / DJs Dan and Andy anyway.

My mucker, my wingman, Lewis, decided that this DJ career wasn't for him, and he hung up the headphones to focus on college at this point and his future training to be a plumber. Sadly, I can't recall how it all happened, the conversation, I mean. Knowing us, I don't think a proper conversation was ever had. Probably just a few teenage grunts whilst playing some darts or pool. Either way, I wasn't bitter, and we didn't fall out with each other. However, I did think that after the millennium gig, it was probably the end for both of us now. Lewis and I were the best of friends anyway, so it wasn't personal. Mind you, thinking back, I can't really blame him. So far, this journey to be a superstar DJs was proving to be fairly stressful. Every gig seemed to present some form of challenge for us, plus he'd probably have much better things to spend all his money on other than random CDs.

Even though the Millennium gig was a stressful

experience and left us, well, me, with zero confidence, we didn't do as bad a job as we thought. We were far too hard on ourselves. In fact, we must have done a good job, because after this, to my surprise, more calls came in and more bookings were made! Legends. The only issue I faced now was that I was a one-man band. I didn't have Lewis/Andy/Ice any more; DJ Ice had melted, and DJ Fire was left extinguished, but as we were in a new year and a new millennium, one door closed and another door opened. Gigs in the Clun Valley still needed a DJ, and who was I to turn my nose up at this? So a naturally adopted 'DJ Dan' was born. The old stage name may have gone, and I'd lost a business partner, but the confidence came back to me, and the fire and passion were relit. I took the Millennium gig as a learning experience, and I was ready for more. Luckily for me, someone else was willing to take the reins and step into Lewis's shoes. Mark, the guy who made me feel stupid at the NYE gig, was enthusiastic, knowledgeable, and ready to step in. Everything seemed to fall into place.

The next gig I took on, I kept my promise to Mark and invited him along to help. If he knew what the coming years were to offer, he'd have probably run a mile at that point and thrown two fingers up at me whilst doing so. All in all, though, everything seemed to work well at the right time, and a smooth transition from Lewis to Mark was made. I just had to get to know him properly now. Dear, God.

Mark. I knew him from school but didn't know him all that personally, if that makes sense. I just knew him from seeing him around school. Mark was in the same year group as me, and his birthday was just two days before mine, so you can tell it was meant to be. I didn't see much of Mark at school as he was in a different form than me, and we didn't share any lessons together. One of us was in a higher group than the other, but I can't remember which one. All I can tell you is that one of us had a normal science class and the other had to do rural science, which is basically a lesson where they don't trust you around classroom chemicals, so, therefore, march you all off down to the school allotment to plant carrots and other varied sources of vegetables and pretend that's actually a lesson to do with science.

Mark also hung around with a different group of friends outside of lessons and during break times. The first time Mark and I first crossed paths, I remember, was in 1994, when we both went on a seventh-grade school trip to France. I, with a few others, shared an apartment, and if my memory serves, he woke up one morning with a squashed banana in his bed, which I strategically placed between his knees whilst he slept, which was a completely normal thing to do—I guess it was one way of 'team building'. The good thing, however, was that he found it highly amusing and continued to let me listen to his 'Now 1994' CD with him on the bus for the rest of the trip. So as you can see, from the beginning, it was destined to be a lifelong friendship. All it took was a foreign country, a squashed banana, and a Now 1994 CD to make that happen. As our school years went on, we lost touch again and drifted apart due to the lessons, forms, and groups we hung around in. However, once secondary school was done and dusted and the school's vegetable patch was full of carrots in 1999, we reconnected at the millennium gig, and I've never been able to shake him off since. Top man, Mark.

It was the year 2000, and our future lay ahead of us; my DJ career was just beginning, and I was full of ambition to attempt to become that top DJ I had always dreamed of being.

Chapter 8
Practice and Patience

As with any new year, it was a year of new beginnings, a new DJ partnership, and learning a new skill—the art of beat mixing, or, as they say, 'proper DJing'. Between the slow and steady gigs and waiting for another to come in from the YFC, we found ourselves willing to accept anything. Mum had already utilised our services; next up, it was my nan. This wasn't to be a full-bore gig, though. This was something far less mental. Nan had booked us on behalf of the WI, or Women's Institute, as they are known, to play an afternoons DJ set beside a pool in the summer sunshine. It was summer, and there was an outdoor swimming pool at a primary school in mid-Wales where Nan and the WI were hosting an afternoon of fundraising.

Think bouncy castles, face painting, coconut shy stalls, and hooking a duck. We were carted over there in the Volvo by mum and presented with a small stage to set up on right next to the tombola. Mark and I got all our kit out and were ready to play an afternoon of god knows what. This wasn't exactly a DJ set, more like background music, really. I can't say for sure that Mark and I were jumping for joy on this one. However, a gig's a gig; after all, how can you turn down any favour your nan asks of you? This was as simple as gigs come and a far cry from the last gig we had done for Millennia, but you wouldn't believe this, though—that gig didn't go totally to plan and had a major downside to it, quite literally, which was by now the complete norm for us. Despite not being the centre of attention, we soon did become the centre of attention when somehow, out of nowhere, there was an almighty bang, and our bloody stage collapsed on us. We went down like the Titanic, and so did all our CDs. They were cast far and wide all over the place after the cases broke, and CDs rolled everywhere. To say this was embarrassing is an understatement. Luckily, though, many good folk came over to lend a hand and retrieve our CDs for us. That was an afternoon I'd rather forget, but it still sticks with me vividly. I thought to myself, I hope when they do the draw on the tombola, I'd best win the bottle of Bells Scotch Whiskey with that 50p I handed over for my ticket. I didn't win the whisky; I won a tin of Del Monte peach halves in syrup instead. What a sucker punch to top the day off.

Now, apart from collapsing stages to the sound of Jim Reeves and winning tinned peaches, I was spending most of, if not all, my spare time in the mix kitchen. The mix kitchen, to put it more simply, was Mum and Dad's spare living room. I put my mind to teaching myself how to DJ properly like a pro and beat mix. Since the departure of Lewis, I had adopted the vinyl turntables from the attic at his mum and dad's house and set them up in the mix kitchen on an old school classroom table salvaged from a skip. I was about to get serious. Although Mark and I were out playing commercial gigs (chart, '80s, party) music, etc., which was great and what the people wanted at gigs, I had always wanted to actually mix, as in beat mix on vinyl (that was the only option at the time), just like Dave Cornish did and the top DJs on BBC Radio 1, the likes of Judge Jules, Dave Pearce, and Pete Tong, to name a few.

I always listened to how they mixed and transitioned between tracks and found it fascinating. When I listened to all the mix CDs we had and live broadcasts on BBC Radio 1, I wasn't just listening to the music that was playing. I was also listening to the actual mix/transition between tracks. Then, when I first-hand witnessed Dave doing it, there was no doubt about it; I wanted to be able to mix too. It was far more advanced than what I'd attempted with The War of the Worlds. Today, technology is so advanced when it comes to DJing, and the skill is far easier to master than it was back in the day when you just put down a piece of black plastic on a turntable and had to read the grooves in a dimly lit DJ booth. When you think back, it makes you wonder how it was even possible. If you're a digital DJ reading this and have never played on a set of vinyl turntables, I urge you to give it a go. It's a million miles away from what it is today. It'll feel a bit like driving a car with no brakes and will undoubtedly test your patience and skill.

I set aside the jukebox cast-offs and started to collect a new collection of vinyl, which was again far more difficult back then than it is today. I remember a simple photocopied, stapled booklet that I got from somewhere, which was from a record shop called Hard To Find Records. In this little book, there was page after page of vinyl listed to order. Of course, you had to know your music to order a record, and there were no websites to go on and have a preview listen of the track before you bought it; you just had to try and figure out a track by its name or be lucky enough that a DJ would name the track they played on the radio. Of course, there were ways you could listen to a record before you bought it in record shops like Virgin Megastore, but when you're a young lad that couldn't drive and was a long way from a big town, you had to make do. The way I got around this eventually was to keep buying any new club mix CD that was released and use those as track references. Once I had all the tracks that I wanted off of that, it was back to gambling for tracks again by their title. I landed on some belters but ended up with even more whoppers. Faux Par.

Out of every 10 records bought, judging by the title, I'd say that at least three of them were good enough to play and practise with, and so with that, I started to teach myself how to beat mix. I had no idea, not a clue, where to start or how to do it other than try to match two beats together and hope for the best. Forget knowing your mix points, BPM, key, time remaining and time elapsed, phrase mixing, and the structure of a dance track. I was a complete novice. Again, 'back in the day', there was no option of going on YouTube to watch tutorials, you may have found something written somewhere on the dial-up internet after you waited six weeks for it to connect and kicked your mum, dad, or sister off the phone to whoever she was courting at the time, but still, I'm certain back then there wasn't anything in the form of video tutorials. The best source of info around at the time and yesterday's Google was Encarta 95, which I don't think had a section on the art of DJing, although it did have a fascinating article on David Bowie with a sound clip, which I found very educational and entertaining—I never got bored of that. Nevertheless, with all the challenges in front of me, I was spending all my money on new records each week, some I knew and many I didn't, and laying down the gauntlet, thinking this time next week I'll be doing BBC Radio 1's Essential Mix. I might have slightly underestimated that a little. To say it was difficult was an understatement; I personally found it extremely difficult. I spent hours and hours trying to crack it but to no avail, but I wasn't going to be defeated. I loved the challenge, and a challenge it certainly was. I ruined many of Mum's Sunday night episodes of Heartbeat whilst she sat down to watch that with the bass lines of Underworld's Born Slippy accompanying it from next door.

I did have know that direct-drive turntables were better than belt-driven turntables and that Technics 1210 decks were the best decks you could buy, equivalent to today's Pioneer CDJ 3000s of the digital world. There was no way I could have ever afforded a pair of those, so I had to make do with my pair of unbranded belt-driven turntables, which made the whole experience double as hard. I did, though—saved my money from gigs and bought a pair of Sound Lab DLP-32s direct drive turntables, but despite being silver, direct driven, and very smart to look at at an affordable cost, they didn't turn me into Paul Van Dyk over night.

Now, then, things were about to change a little, and I was in luck for a change. Dave Cornish, I'll always remember, had a turntable set up in his living room at his house over in Newtown, Mid Wales; it was a Technics 1210 MK2, to be precise, and he used to get promos sent to him by record labels for free, and this is where he'd listen to them. Promos were something that I could only dream of receiving through the post—free music! Record companies, however, would only send these to fully established working DJs, and at this point, I had no hope of getting some sent to me. So, for now, any vinyl that came delivered to me was bought. Dave had a vast collection of records, as you can imagine, after receiving vinyl for years. When working with him, I told him I was trying to beat mix, but just like a song by the Climax Blues Band, I couldn't get it right. I couldn't get anything right other than the speed at which the record had to play.

As if Dave hadn't already helped me enough with my journey as Captain Chaos so far, he, in his down time on evenings and the odd weekends, told me what I should be doing and where I was going wrong. Then, when that still didn't sink in and work, and I spent a lot of time on the phone with him in a bad temper, he kindly offered to show me the basics and give me some tutorial time on beat mixing. Dave then became my personal, professional tutor. He'd become my real-life YouTube.

I'd go over to his place at the weekend, and he'd show me a mix completed by him, then I'd jump on the decks and show him a train wreck. After laughing and putting his head in his hands, he'd then give me some pointers on where I was going wrong and guide me towards the correct way. I'll always remember him being very patient with me and never getting fed up with me sounding like a jackhammer in his front room, which was remarkable as I was ready to throw myself out of his house many times.

As I mentioned before, I was just starting to build a vinyl collection, and I didn't have many records at the time. The ones I did have, I was absolutely fed up with, as I'd heard them over and over again. It really was a good way of destroying your love for a track. Dave, as I said, had a vast collection of records he'd bought over the years and the many promos he was receiving too. He had his spare room upstairs, absolutely stacked floor to ceiling with vinyl. It was a magnificent sight, and it looked like a stock room in a music shop.

One weekend when I was at his, he kindly let me go through his entire collection and said I could take any record I wanted and add it to my collection to build it up. Unbelievable act of kindness this was. I thought he was joking, but he wasn't. I was like a kid in a sweet shop—no, I was like a kid in a record shop that was able to take whatever I wanted. I remember being polite and only taking a small handful; when he saw what I had taken, he said that I was never going to be able to play a set with that few and said to go and get some more! This was what Dave was like: he had a heart of gold, was incredibly kind, and really went out of his way to help me and many other young budding local DJs in the same situation as me at the time. He always had time and patience for all of us.

Just quickly, though, and completely irrelevant—but different enough that I'd just like to mention it before I forget and never get a chance to say it again—Dave wouldn't drink coffee or tea in the morning. He'd always have a cup of hot water. To this day, I've never met anyone else who would find a cup of hot water in the morning satisfying; somehow, Dave did. Each to their own, I guess. Odd.

So, let's get back to the mix kitchen. I had vinyl aplenty now that Dave had kindly donated a stack to me. I spent uncountable hours trying desperately and tirelessly to get to grips with beat matching and implement everything he had taught me so far. The struggle and frustration were real, but practise and patience was the key to success. I never gave up, and then one day, all that practise and patience finally started to pay off, and with that, just like a track I had on vinyl by System F, out of the blue, I got a successful mix, then another, and another! It finally clicked. Somehow, the pieces started to fall into place, and I started to figure out how to do it. Like riding a bike, I suppose. I was over the moon. They weren't perfect, but I was getting closer and closer. I practised and practised over and over again, making sure it wasn't just a fluke, but no, it finally made sense, and from this point on, just like Forrest Gump when he went out for a run, I just kept on mixing.

Chapter 9
Mysterious Times

With the basics of beat matching in place, now wasn't the time to get complacent with it. Every spare moment I had, I continued to practise for as many hours as I could. I was driving my mum and dad bonkers with their spare room doubling up as a stock room and a nightclub. I was in there, shut away like a hermit, mixing away, trying to polish up the skills so they were good enough for the next Ministry of Sound Annual CD. There was an old wardrobe in which I used to store all my records. I once wrote 'DJ Dan in the Mix' on it, just next to my decks. My dad, being the comedian he was, decided that one day he'd vandalise it by writing underneath 'As Always'. I never figured out what he meant by that. Was it because I was always in there mixing? Or was he suggesting I was puddled? Knowing Dad, it was probably the latter. Plank.

We're still in 2000, and with the steady flow of gigs now coming in and Mark now a solid business partner with me on them, it was fair to say that we now had new foundations for what will hopefully be a successful new DJ business. We were now getting booked to DJ many more YFC gigs in the valley as well as branching out to do birthday parties and weddings, which was good news for us. Weekends got busy with our gigs now, so unfortunately, I had to take a step back from riding out with Dave on his gigs. Dave didn't mind one bit, though; he was pleased that things were progressing for us. Dave was always very supportive and was always on hand to offer advice or hire extra equipment when needed.

So, with a new business underway, there was one key thing missing: a new name. We needed something a little more than Dan and Mark or DJ Dan. One day, from somewhere very imaginative, we adopted the title 'Mystikal Productions'. The 'Productions' part came from looking at Dave's business, which was called Red Flame Productions, so I thought if it was good enough for him, then it was good enough for us. The 'Mystikal' part, no matter how hard I try to think, I cannot remember where I dug that up from. Did you notice it was spelt with a K in it? I'll hold my hand up; that was me that did that. It stands out a little more, doesn't it? Looks better on a poster. Unfortunately, my creative mind didn't think that; it came about because my spelling wasn't all that good, and I thought it was spelt with a 'K'. Nevertheless, it stayed. Well, until we did actually get our name on posters, then the clever people spelt it the right way, 'Mystical', which then looked wrong and misspelt. I did then think to spell it properly, but I did prefer the K, and we had promotional material knocked up by then, so we had no choice but to leave it in place.

We did, however, end up on posters of all sorts. Mystikal Productions, Mystical Productions, and the classic DJ Dan, but the best I once saw has to be when the gig we were doing made it into the local paper. I remember my dad was sitting at the kitchen table and couldn't wait until we came in to say that us two 'prannies' were in the newspaper. Mark and I were made up, and we looked at each other with huge proud smiles on our faces until I saw we were labelled up as 'DJ Dan and his Mystical Experience'. What the bloody hell was that all about!? Don't get me wrong, we were extremely grateful we got a mention; I just didn't want to mislead people into thinking myself and my 'Mystical Experience' were rolling into town on Saturday night with a convoy of waggons packed full of wild, exotic animals and fire breathers or leave people thinking they were going to get a night of jaw-dropping illusions. Mind you, that fog machine we had from Dave was strong and thick enough to make anything disappear for about 10 to 15 minutes.

Anyway, with my dad absolutely loving this title and making his year and no doubt taking the clipping down to the pub to show everyone how proud he was of us, all spelling aside and newly turning out as many new identities, Mark and I were officially Mystikal Productions.

Chapter 10
Walking the Mile

Still, in 2000 (a long year), neither of us had driving licences and couldn't drive (legally). We weren't 17 until June of that year, so we couldn't even start driving lessons. Not exactly handy when you're a pair of budding artists getting booked for gigs but can't drive. So, for now, the transport was kindly and, at the same time, reluctantly provided by Mum and the trusty Volvo 740 GLE. Perhaps this is what the paper meant by DJ Dan and his Mystical Experience? Turning up to play a gig in a clapped-out Volvo estate by his long-suffering mum, who knows?

We had gigs coming in, but luckily for us, having no driving licences, the gigs were local, either two miles up the road in the Newcastle on Clun village hall, where I got my big break, or three miles down the road in the other direction at the Clun Memorial Hall, where we pieced together the millennium gig. This was handy for Mum as I don't think after a long, hard week at work, spending the weekend ferrying equipment around for us was on her list of things to do, so at least she only had a 10-minute drive to the venue, which was also handy for us, because once that last piece of equipment came out of the boot of the Volvo, the car was gone. Imagine leaning into the boot of a car and grabbing hold of a box, and then the car moves out of the way, and you are left there holding it in the same position. That's what it was like, just like a sketch from a comedy on TV. Mum didn't seem to hang around too long, and once we had finished setting up, we had a nice two-mile scenic walk home and a nice summer's evening walk back to the gig at night. Then a nice summer's morning walk back home again after the gig. We were fit lads at 17. However, Mum would fire up the Volvo and spring back into action the next day to ferry the equipment back to the storage facility in the front room; she just wasn't keen on the graft in-between. No stamina.

The Volvo would carefully be parked up on a grass verge

on the edge of a narrow road on a bend, and Mark and I would haul the gear out of the boot, dodge the traffic on that bend, go up some narrow steps through the garden gate, all the way up the stretch of a long garden, through the porch, smashing our knuckles on the door frame and into the hub, It was by no means practical, safe, or easy to load and unload that gear, but as I said, we were young and fit from all our walking. It was all change, though. By June 2000, Mark and I were both proud driving licence holders, and although this was brilliant for us and a long time coming, unfortunately, the first thing that had to be done as a business was a tough decision. Mum was made redundant, which she didn't seem to be bothered about, and things didn't kick off. She did demand a pay-out, though, for all the fuel she had to put in the Volvo to run us around. To my memory, and to save it from going to court, I think we settled on £15. She could have gotten £20 if she had completed the journeys with us actually getting a lift home. Court adjourned.

With legal proceedings all taken care of, Mum was made redundant, but the Volvo was still in action, and I was reluctantly given the key. I think in the end, I had to round up that £15 to £20 to get that key to the silver tank. During the week, it was Mum's car for work, and come the weekend, the back seats were dropped, and anything that remained in the boot was cast out and onto the driveway in all weathers, and it became our workhorse. We were now officially mobile DJs, at long last. This was good news as business was booming and we were spreading our wings; we had now got bookings for more parties and weddings coming in, which were further afield than our current 4-mile radius. Walking six miles a day for a gig was quite enough, and we could finally not have to think about packing a can of Lynx Atlantis in our kit for after our walk.

Now, with wedding gigs, much like birthdays, this came with a little extra pressure as it meant collecting a vast back catalogue of music ranging from the '60s all the way up to the present. We had all the current music but were a little depleted with an older selection of music. But that wasn't too much of an issue. Once more, the Volvo estate was fired up and took to the hills to descend on

Woolworths again to raid their sales bins for old music CDs. There was no doubt that we were the best customers they had.

Driving 40 minutes to a shop to buy a mass amount of CDs for a gig may sound a bit long-winded and quite an effort these days, and I'll agree with that. Thinking about it now, it was an effort, but there weren't any easier alternatives then. Downloading music wasn't available back then; there was downloading available if you had the patience to wait a week for one song to download, with the risk of your computer being completely destroyed by viruses and rendered scrap afterward. It was quicker to drive to the shop and back than it was to download a four-minute track.

When we were given what the bride and groom wanted for their first dance, we had to pray and hope it was on a CD we had because, if it wasn't...? You guessed it; we'd be back in Woolworths looking through every CD compilation to see if it had the song on, and if it did, we'd have to pay, what, £10 for that CD just for that song! Absolutely crazy when you think back really to the extreme levels you had to go to. That's probably why I had quite a large collection of CDs in no time.

Another thing with gigs, especially weddings, was that we needed to look smart. We couldn't just turn up in rough jeans and T-shirts, could we? No, so that's why we bought the best black faux silk shirts a tenner could buy and shipped them off to the printers to get our business name printed on the back and our names on the left-hand side chest area, just in case people forgot who we were or really needed to know. In fact, I can remember those smart shirts we had; they were from Burton, they had a silky feel to them, and they were finished off with a smart velvety red Chinese dragon on one side of the chest. Lads, you'll remember this style from then; everyone had them, I think? Or they were so dreadful that only we could get them. Anyway, we also completed the look with a smart grey tie with a picture of two decks and a mixer on. I found these at the same time in a bargain bin and couldn't get them could I, a bit of us they were. When we turned up at a wedding, we didn't half look smart as carrots; we meant business and made a statement. Professional planks at your service, trying our best not to ruin the soundtrack to your special day.

Chapter 11
All the Gear and Some Ideas

Let's now head to 2002. The past two years as a new duo, Mystikal Productions. Mark and I were busy grown-up 19-year-olds, both now holding down full-time day jobs—well, Mark was holding down his, and I struggled. This occupied us during the week, and at weekends, we were either out doing gigs or discussing the next gig in our office, the White Horse pub in Clun. Our gigs were unrepentantly expanding rapidly inside and outside the area. Different YFC clubs throughout the county were booking us for dances in village halls and barns, and in between these, we could be found sporting our posh faux silk shirts at weddings and birthday parties. The YFC gigs were getting bigger—much bigger. We were finding ourselves on farms in huge barns and warehouses now, and with this, we needed more power—lighting- and sound-wise. We were beginning to spend more time in barns than with livestock and hay bales.

By this time, we'd started to invest heavily in new equipment, which was wise as our original setup was pretty lethal and about as insurable as a camper van pitched on a river bank in flood season. We had scrapped the metal curtain poles and masking tape holding up the lighting for proper lighting stands and trusses; through Dave, we managed to get some new speakers and an amplifier on finance, and we finally told Dave that we would no longer require the fog machine and got one of our own that was actually safe to use. We had also started updating all the lighting we had. Our pay packets each month were taking a pounding with the amount we were spending on equipment, and with every gig we did, we invested that money straight back into even more equipment. Our empire was growing, and the living room at Mum and Dad's was absolutely stacked floor to ceiling.

One thing about Mark and me is that we both didn't do things by halves. We were both as picky and precise as each other, which was good. For example, if we couldn't buy one new light, we'd have to have a pair. If we needed three, we'd have four, and so on. And this was the general rule of thumb for everything. Each setup we had had to be symmetrical to look at, and with this outlook, equipment doubled quickly. We took a lot of pride in how the setup would look when switched on and when just set up without doing anything.

Luckily for us, Dave always had our backs. With the bigger gigs we did, we needed much bigger speakers, as we were both obsessed with feeling the music and hearing it. Dave had a huge stack of powerful speakers, and we always hired these off of him for our 'big' gigs, along with the odd piece of lighting that we didn't yet own ourselves. The speakers always came packed into a custom-made trailer to tow them too, which was extremely handy and something we loved. So much so that we bought it off Dave a few years later—not the speakers, the trailer. Dave did give us a quote once for a set of speakers we hired. He casually handed us the quote on paper he'd written up. We saw £10,000 on it and casually handed it straight back to him whilst he looked on with a huge grin, thinking, I think you lads will still be customers for a while yet. He wasn't wrong there.

Unfortunately, though, the time came for another redundancy. I'm sad to report that this time it was the trusted Volvo. She had served us well, but we had outgrown her boot, and it joined Mum in retirement from Mystikal Productions. This was a relief in a way, though, as it meant that I didn't have to listen to my dad telling us anymore that we've overloaded it again and I'm going to break the suspension on it. He loved standing there with a cup of coffee and a fag on the go, watching us grunt whilst we crammed the equipment into it. Of course, naturally, by him saying we've overloaded, it wasn't going to stop us from taking all the equipment we wanted. We didn't care; it was only when that car had every square inch of space filled, the boot was shut, and we were ready to go. It was then, when we drove off with the exhaust catching the driveway, looking like we had strapped some sparklers to it, and the bonnet of the car was up in the air and felt more like I was steering a ship on choppy waters, that I thought perhaps Dad was right. But we had a gig to get to.

But that was a problem in the past anyway, as I'd made a new purchase. I was now the proud owner of an M-Reg Ford Transit van, complete with a Goodman's tape player and a generous amount of rust. I bought this van at a very cheap mate's rates from my mate Lewis—well, his dad, Brian. Brian let me have it cheap as he was upgrading to a new van, and I'm pretty sure this one I paid scrap value for. In fact, I think that's where it was heading anyway, the scrap yard. I was as proud as punch.

Mark was, and still is a Land Rover enthusiast and drove around in a classic Series 2 Land Rover Defender, which was ideal as we had some storage room in the back of his Defender to cart equipment around in, and when we hired the big stack of speakers off Dave for the big gigs, Mark could just hook up the trailer effortlessly and drive away, so Mark was the man to tow that gig to gig. I do remember that because we had no spare money for anything else other than equipment and CDs, a sign-written vehicle was not in the budget, so again, in our true fashion to improvise, we grabbed a roll of black insulation tape out of Mark's dashboard and sign-wrote the side of his Land Rover ourselves. I think it was just for a laugh initially, but we did leave it on there to go to the gig.

With Mark's Land Rover beautifully sign-written in tape, I closely followed behind in my transit. It's fair to say we had a beautiful convoy, a sight to behold when coming up a posh drive to a wedding venue, a Land Rover that hadn't seen a hose pipe since the day it rolled off the production line, and a trailer that had enough things growing on it. It looked like a mobile science experiment, not to mention a van that looked like it would leave most of itself at the venue when we left. I often contemplated putting a dustpan and brush in that van to brush up the rust off the ground after you had shut the door. I'd have put that next to the bag of sawdust that was carried around to throw on the oil leak once the van was moved. I still loved her, though. The dirty workhorse.

Everything was coming together nicely, nice new gear, our own transport, which was something to be desired, and one and a half heads of knowledge about what we were doing.

Mark was extremely clever with electrics and generally anything I was rubbish at, which is more than you'd think. Mark was one of these annoyingly clever people who just knew how to do pretty much everything and anything. We all know someone like that. He was just an information hoover. I knew my music and did the DJing, but when it came to wiring up all the sound and lighting, I wasn't much help at all; if it couldn't be plugged into an extension lead and switched on, I was lost. I was okay with small, basic setups, but the big setups got a little too advanced and overwhelming for me, what with all the DMX lighting and whatnot. I was a grafter, though. I'd get my head down, my arse up, and graft good. I'd help get all the equipment out of the vehicles and into place, and Mark would cable it all up and get it working. If I got too involved, cocked something up, or generally interfered, which I did much more than I should have, ultimately getting in Mark's way and pushing his buttons, you'd often hear him shout, "For Christ's sakes, don't think...just jock!"

When I heard those words come out of his mouth, I'd go and sort my CDs, look over my shoulder, and tell him how clever he was. If he was in a right stinker with me, all I'd have to do to get him back onside was start playing a track that he liked. As soon as I saw his foot tapping, I knew it was safe to start interfering again.

Chapter 12
Bang The Stage Again!

2002 was the year that, along with my dream of being a superstar DJ, I went out to achieve my second dream of being a firefighter. I remember having the conversation with Mum and Dad and saying that this was something that I really wanted to do. Mum and Dad both knew a local builder, Graham Dudley, who was a firefighter in the local area of Clun, and they called him, saying I was interested in joining up. In fact, it was a little earlier than this, as I remember putting in my application a few weeks before I was 18 years old. Anyway, come 2002, after Graham had invited me down to the fire station in Clun to attend some drill nights and helped me with my application, my application was approved, and I began my training as a firefighter in August of 2002 for the Shropshire Fire and Rescue Service, which I was immensely proud to be joining.

With training underway to become a firefighter, we went back to the gigs, and another YFC gig was upon us, so preparation started early. As I said before, by now we had quite a lot of equipment in our hands, and Mark and I certainly didn't do things by half. It was all or nothing with us by now.

We had seriously expanded from our original setup, thankfully, but we still didn't have all the lighting we really wanted. We weren't huge fans and weren't really impressed with standard 'spinning' disco lights. We wanted a more 3D light show—something different, something that you'd see in the clubs, lasers, scanners, moving heads, etc., lighting that had the wow factor. Thing is, although this kind of lighting is fairly cheap these days, back then, it was big money—way too much for us. One piece of equipment we always wanted and strived for was a good laser. In 2002, lasers were used in big nightclubs and would have cost the same amount as a house; they were probably the same size as one. Lasers on the mobile scene weren't really out there yet—not the amazing ones, anyway; they were coming through slowly, but you'd need a mortgage to buy a good one.

However, all was not lost. One night, over a pint in The White Horse, Mark pulled out a rolled-up magazine from the inside of his denim jacket, and what was in there? Not the magazine I thought he was pulling out; it was a Maplin electronics magazine, which he must have found much more exciting than I did. That was until he presented me with an offer on two lasers; needless to say, for a jaw-dropping £60, we couldn't turn our noses up at these. We couldn't believe our luck here—£60 for two lasers to add to our set up. I don't know what we were expecting for £60, but it was certainly different from our thoughts of a laser so powerful and bright it would take the village hall roof off.

Now, no matter how much I try to work this out, I can't. The night before this particular gig, we got the keys to the Clun Memorial Hall from the caretakers, Dilys and John, who were a lovely couple in the village. We went down to the village hall to make a start on setting up our new, expanded setup. Why!? Compared to later years, this setup was a pop-up disco. Personally, the only reason I can think of is that we were just too excited to get the new bargain lasers out of the boxes to try them. I mean, we tried them at home in the living room as soon as they arrived, which was okay. You could see the pattern on the wall, which looked like a drunk person having a go with that Spirograph game you had as a child. Just a mass of squiggly lines moving all over the place whilst it sent our Jack Russell dog, Flo, absolutely scatty. But lighting just wasn't lighting without some 'atmos' as Mark liked to call it, which was fog from the fog machine to me and you. This really brought lighting out in its best form. The trouble was, having already commandeered the living room at Mum and Dad's full of equipment, I didn't want to rock the boat and fill the house with fog too. I felt that may just push them that bit too far over the edge, well, Mum, anyway, as dad usually went off down the pub—or 'The Legion', as Mark would say to him—and in return would be given some form of rude hand gesture coupled with some fowl words.

We descended on the Clun Memorial Hall at 7:00 p.m. and set about getting the rig in place. The reason I know it was 7:00 p.m. is because I actually have camcorder video footage of this. At the time, I was working in an electrical shop called Currys, which later became Currys - PC World. I worked in the Newtown branch, which was very handy as it was only a few doors down from our Woolworths. I used to have to wear a pastel yellow shirt for my uniform, which delighted my dad, as he always took great pleasure in calling me Primrose and never got bored of entertaining himself with that.

I remember I got the camcorder cheap as it was marked up wrong, and from then on, we started filming our gigs, which was exciting; we were vlogging! Long before the vloggers of today knew what vlogging was or before vlogging was actually a thing.

So, with the lighting up, which included the bargain lasers, it was time to fire up the fog machine and see what the lasers had to offer. In our minds, this was going to blow the crowd away with what we've got here, which it would have done if you could have seen them. They were, in two words, totally useless. Today's laser pens have more power than they did; in fact, they were so useless that you couldn't even see them through the fog! You had to wait until that dissipated before they shone through, but at the time, if you saw the camcorder footage, we were in awe of them. We loved them; you can clearly hear our excitement in the footage, which is hilarious. Take my word for it.

The lighting was set up. We had three moonflower effect lights that were sound-activated on the stage, meaning they'd rotate to music via their built-in microphone. Only having three of them did annoy us slightly; when we had the music on testing, the lighting all worked; we were too busy to keep an eye on anything else other than the lasers, but we needed to check these three moon flowers were up to scratch and worked before we went home for the evening. The sound had been unplugged, so we had to do things manually—well, Mark did. I was a cameraman at this point, so I was filming this extravaganza of a light show unfolding in front of us; these lights were just shining away and not moving because there was no sound. "Mark!" I shouted. "Go to the stage and get those lights to move!" With his great big, size-16 feet, there was a huge thud that sounded like the stage was collapsing, and they all sprang into life, so just to make sure I'd captured this moment on video, I shouted back to Mark,"Bang the stage again!" And that became a regular test for us. Mark always bangs the stage or taps the internal microphones on the lights.

Chapter 13
In the Wrong Place at the Right Time

2003 came with a change of circumstances. This year, I fled the nest at Mum and Dad's and finally became a proper man with my own house. I rented a house in Clun, mainly because it got me closer to the fire station to respond to call-outs or 'shouts', as they are known, and of course I knew everything I needed to know about work and finances, so it was a good time to put that into practise whilst ignoring all the good advice I was given prior to it. I moved into this house with a good friend of mine, Al. Al was quite a character—a modern-day Jesus because he had long hair and was of a slim build—and very inventive. Al was a very clever lad, though; he was a good carpenter, a brilliant guitarist, and an even better drinker.

We had a right good time living in that house, and Jack, the landlord at the White Horse pub, well, his profits soon doubled when Al moved to the village of Clun. Paying the rent was cheap and cheerful. Each and every Friday, Al and I had to pop, I think, £35 cash into a Truprint photograph order envelope (minus the film) with a little note book, which was our rent book, and drop it through the letterbox of our landlord Eric's house on the way around to the pub, and the next morning it was returned through our letterbox ready for the following week. Eric was a lovely man; the only reason he let a couple of young idiots rent his house was that he knew I was new to the fire service, and he used to be the Sub Officer, the man in charge of the station, years ago at the same fire station, so he was helping me out there. Upon my interview for the house, I remember him asking me all sorts of questions and finishing by asking me if I liked to drink. I didn't know what to reply with. Was he trying to figure out whether it was going to be a noisy frat house? I was honest and said yes, "I do like the 'odd pint'." "Good. Because I don't trust any man who doesn't drink," he replied. And with that, I was handed my photograph envelope and notepad. What a lovely man Eric was.

Back to the gigs: oddly enough, our luck was and had been on our side for quite some time with our gigs, but it was only a matter of time before something went Pete Tong. We had another Local YFC gig penned in on a Saturday night at the Clun Memorial Hall, this time though we had ditched the idea of going down the night before to set up as that was getting silly, and after the last effort with the lasers, it was a bit of an anti-climax. Besides, by now we had discovered that most normal people go to a place they called a 'pub' at the weekend and certainly not fannying around in a village hall, so we attempted to be normal and head there instead for our usual pint and prawn crackers, just waiting until Mark put a quid in the juke box and played KLF... again.

Mark and I went down to the memorial hall on Saturday mid-afternoon to get all set up and ready for the night that lay ahead. Even though we stopped going to the venue the night before to set up, we would always get in as early as we could on the day of the event, so it would give us plenty of time should something not go to plan. We finished the setup, went home, and chilled for a bit before heading back out to the gig via a quick pit stop in the White Horse to get a feel for how many folks were out and about and coming to the gig. This was common practise for us when we did gigs at the Clun Memorial Hall, as with no real progress on social media, you had no idea how many folk were out and about. We got through the doors of the White Horse at about 7:30 p.m. for a quick drink and recce before the doors to the village hall opened at 8:00 p.m.

I remember us being a little disappointed when we walked into the pub this time. There was hardly anyone there. I mean, the pub was always busy, but when there was a gig down the village hall, the White Horse burst at the seams. However, not tonight? This wasn't right, surely? On an evening of a gig at the memorial hall, you'd normally hear everyone in good spirits before you'd even got to the pub, and you'd struggle to push your way through to the bar to get a drink. On this particular evening, there was no noise upon arrival at the pub, and as soon as we walked in, we could head straight to the bar without a wet sleeve. Anyhow, Mark and I finished our pints, put all negativity aside, and walked the five-minute walk down to the village hall. Things got a little stranger than the quiet pub situation when we walked into the memorial hall car park and up to the doors. The village hall was all in darkness, there wasn't a single car parked in the car park, and the doors were locked shut. This confused us both now, and coupled with the lack of anyone in the pub, obviously, something wasn't tallying up, which started to make us worry.

The good thing is, it wasn't long before the answers to a dark and quiet village hall came to light, and when they did, it came delivered like a fiercely swinging wrecking ball straight between the legs. My phone rang; it was the person who had booked us for the gig. I looked at Mark, and Mark looked at me as they were put on loudspeakers. They were politely asking where we were and why we weren't set up yet. Both of us looked at each other, mightily confused. The organiser continued to say that the doors were open and people were arriving, but we weren't there. All we could see was a dark village hall and an empty parking lot. The penny dropped, and we knew there and then that we had made a monumental cock up. "Oh, bother!" we both shouted out; what a pickle we seem to be in.

We, Mark and I, the professional planks, had somehow only managed to set up for the gig on the right day—the small matter was, in the wrong village hall! So we were well and truly in the wrong place at the right time. We were all set up in the Clun Memorial Hall when we actually needed to be set up in the Newcastle Village Hall, four miles up the road! The organiser, after explaining to them where we were and what had happened, was quite panicked, as anyone would be when the DJ you've booked for your gig is standing in a dark village hall car park on a Saturday night. We assured him that we would be there asap to rectify this minor issue. Once we had gotten off the phone with the organiser and stopped sounding like a brass band tuning up for a concert, we ran to the caretaker's house as fast as we could, grabbing lamp posts as we turned corners, grabbed the keys to the memorial hall, ran back, packed all the gear down in record time, threw it—and I mean threw it—into the van. Equipment was getting launched into the van with cables still attached to them, knocking even more rust off the panels, and got up to the correct village hall to set up all over again.

This was an awful, gut-wrenching experience, not to mention highly embarrassing! We were lugging gear onto the stage through the fire exit and settting up whilst people were pouring in through the main entrance, ready to dance the night away! Thank God the bar was open and kept the masses occupied whilst Laurel and Hardy sorted themselves out. Mark thought fast and said to get the decks plugged in and a CD playing while we set up the rest of the rig. Smart move. There was certainly no time tonight for a bench test by banging the stage! People were coming in expecting some music, but all they could hear for the first 10 minutes was a disgusting amount of bad language and us throwing the gear onto the stage, sounding like a bin waggon tipping bottles into it.

All was soon forgotten, though, after about half an hour, when the lights came on to accommodate the music. But I cannot tell you how paranoid about future gigs this made me. I never wanted a repeat of that night ever again. Although we were lucky in one respect, the village halls were only about four miles apart from each other, and it was a small rig setup. I couldn't imagine how much more of a disaster that could have been if it was one of our large rig setups, miles away from each other, or even worse, a wedding. I still don't quite understand how Dilys and John, the caretakers of the Memorial Hall, gave us the keys to set up and didn't know themselves that there was no event that evening. Mind you, Mark and I did treat it like a second home and were always in and out of that place like a woodpecker's nose; they probably just trusted us a little too much to know what we were doing.

So that gig was a near disaster, which could have potentially cost us lots of future gigs because of a lack of professionalism; from then on, I made a special trip to W.H. Smiths, cleared the stationary shelves, and set up an office in my spare room at my house. Proper gig booking sheets were printed and used to record every confirmed gig, not just written down with an Argos pencil on the back of the Yellow Pages in-between the skip hire and electricians advert. We could not afford to mess up again, ever! Oddly enough, though, we did, one night, totally redeem ourselves from that incident. Something quite strange happened...

The same guy who organised that night we messed up on must have got the right hump with us after that fowl up, which you can't blame him for. He had organised another gig at the Newcastle village hall some months later but had swerved our services and booked someone else, another DJ, which was no great surprise to us.

I remember it was a Saturday night, about 8:30 p.m., and for once, Mark and I were having a rare weekend off. My phone rang, and it was this guy, the organiser of the gigs, in a fit of panic, which was becoming normal to me, although even though I was home having a quiet one, I still thought, What the bloody hell have we done now? The organiser had rung me to tell me that the other DJ he had booked for this gig was a no-show, and we could please spring into action and save the night! Well, my first thoughts were that perhaps this other DJ had gotten the wrong venue too, as it has already been proven that it was an easy mistake to make, but then I thought that no one else would have been as ill-prepared as us. I wanted to ask him, "Have you checked the Clun Memorial Hall car park?" But I thought against it at this particular moment, as it would have no doubt added fuel to the fire. I always liked a challenge; this was a golden opportunity to save the day, get us back in, and keep us in the good books with this particular YFC club. I accepted and agreed that we would be there ASAP, although Mark didn't know that yet. Gigs at Newcastle village hall started to get very rushed and fast-paced.

I called Mark up and explained the situation, and of course, he was pleased and was only too happy to get out of his pyjamas, switch off Dr. Who, throw on his double denim attire, and make the 30 minute-journey over to the storage facility to load the rust bucket up and do a gig last minute.

My memory isn't always the best; however, on
this particular night, I could tell you that one four-letter
word was used an awful lot, which became fairly standard
when he saw me ring.

The evening was saved, though; Mark and I arrived once
more, fashionably late, at the Newcastle village hall in the
mobile skip and the defender, having to frantically explain
to everyone hurling abuse that this time was not our fault
and that we were the heroes this time. We took it all on the
chin like a couple of winners and set about getting the
partygoers going. After many pints of warm Worthing
Cream Flow served in plastic pint pots and Bacardi
Breezers served to the masses, our late arrival to the party
was soon forgotten once more, and we proudly played on
into the night. I'm also pleased to report that this act of
commitment on this night to the YFC club did get us back
in the good books for future gigs with them, and they then
started booking us for all their future events. Well saved.
Cheers.

Chapter 14
Have fun and party

Dave Cornish was always at hand, as I explained earlier. He was the backbone and support to our larger gigs. We just about scraped through the smaller gigs ourselves. We always needed his support right the way through with the sound system for the large gigs, we stopped hiring lighting from him as we'd invested in our own, but the speakers we had off him were always going to be out of our league! Which now, thinking about it, I'm glad we hired them off him each time, as it was nice to stay involved with him.

Dave was a different and unique man; he'd drink warm water, he had a booming and distinct voice, he was always a man on a mission, power walking everywhere double time, and I remember well on every invoice he sent me in the post, or when Mark collected them when picking up equipment, he'd always sign off with 'Have fun and party'. He always signed off with the same, whether it be invoices, emails, texts or calls, wrapping up any form of correspondence with Dave would always be 'Have fun and party' this became his infamous tag line, and everybody would know him for saying that phrase. If you ever said that to someone, they knew that you knew Dave Cornish.

Let's have a look at 2004 now, if we dare. This was an eye-opener for us. Mark and I were in our prime at 21 years old. We thought it was about time we jumped on the bandwagon and did what all DJs do in the summer, including Dave, and head out to Ibiza for a week and get a real insight into it for educational purposes. So with that plan in mind, we set about getting to the party island. We packed our bags, loaded up the iPod with all the latest club bangers, arrived at Birmingham airport, and we boarded a flight to Magaluf instead for a week's holiday with Mark's parents. It was far cheaper; we couldn't have afforded Ibiza. Make no mistake, though, Magaluf was fantastic and jaw-dropping for us, a couple of country bumpkin DJs. We had the time of our lives out there and certainly made the most of it. While Mark's mum and dad (Chris and Kate) went shopping, sightseeing, and relaxing, Mark and I searched for potential night spots to get into, and boy, did we find one. Thanks to promotional people out on the streets, we were handed a flyer which sold us instantly. Judge Jules playing a club called BCM. The entry fee was €20, and drinks were unlimited, who could refuse and offer like that? Certainly not us. Once we went to BCM on the first night, we were blown away by it, and I'm pretty sure that's where we went every night we remained in Magaluf. We spent every night studying it, yes, studying it. Most would be in there to lose the plot for the evening, but not us, well, we did let our hair down, but after some all-important homework first.

We studied everything in that club, from the lighting, lasers, DJ booth, and the DJs, literally right down to the power cables. We lived life on the edge. Now, although you may laugh and us, and if you know us, you will, this was fascinating. We had both never experienced clubbing or clubs before on this level. It was somewhat different to Mr. Evans's barn back in Shropshire.

We studied the place and the equipment that closely. Not even ladies walking around filling up our drinks in a pair of pants for free could divert our attention. We took hundreds of photos on the digital camera at the time. Mark was better at that than me; he had a natural talent for photography and was more attentive to detail than I was. He took pictures of the lights, lasers, and the famous DJs we admired, all in the name of research and seeing what ideas we could take back with us and implement into our business, looking back at them now, though, you'd think we were working in the lingerie business or Ann Summers by the number of pictures of ladies in pants he'd 'accidentally' taken of all the clubs dancers. He still, to this day, vows that it's the lighting behind them is what he was taking a picture of. I believe him.

At this time, we had gotten acquainted with the resident DJ at BCM, who was a decent chap. We talked to him and got friendly with him, probably because we went into the club far too early before it got busy so we could have a good look over the equipment in there. If we had gone in there any earlier, we would have been involved in the staff team briefings. We may have been as dull as dishwater to most, but we didn't care; in my eyes, I was in heaven. Now, on this night, Judge Jules from BBC Radio 1 was playing a set, the judge was one of my favorite DJs, and as you know, I listened to all his shows from the attic years prior. I was properly starstruck to actually see him play live and 10 feet in front of me. There was a track that Judge Jules was playing on his shows on radio 1 at the time that I could not get for love or money, it must have been a white label.

He played it there while we were watching his DJ set; after he played it and was putting it back in his CD folder, fuelled by cheap vodka and orange juice and trusted enough to be in close quarters, I had the brass neck to ask him if I could have the CD. And do you know what, with a smile, he handed over that very CD to me, just like that! Unbelievable! I still have that to this very day. The track, if you wanted to know, was called 'Be Free With Your Love (Fonzerelli Remix)' by Miami Dub Machine. When I think back to this first trip away to Magaluf with Mark's parents, With what we were doing with the Djing and the movie of Kevin and Perry Go Large, we were actually living that reality! Mark's mum and dad even came out to BCM one or two of the nights. Absolutely classic.

All raved out and many SD cards full of pants, Myself and Hugh Hefner were back in Blighty, and we're now in 2005, and this year was the year that things started to snowball and pick up pace. We were soon filling the calendar with dates at weekends. Mark was full-time employed, I was employed, unemployed, redundant, part-time or having a well-earned break from the graft and whatever other excuse I could find not to hold down a job for more than 24 hours. We were partying like it was 1999 and attended more weddings to provide the soundtrack than reverends had read vows. Although my work was varied, by 2005, I had been a retained firefighter for three years, so to date, that had been the longest job I'd ever held down, which was an achievement in itself, but that was one of my life's dreams so I was content there. Mark was very proud of me and told me all the time how proud he was of me, he didn't really, but I knew he was. I joined the fire service in 2002, so that was one tick off my list of what I wanted to do when I left school; the other was to become a DJ, which I was having a good crack at, and the third was to become a radio presenter, which we will come to soon.

2005-2008 I personally think, were incredible years for us and for our gigs. We were in our prime, building the most advanced mobile entertainment business, music at that time was incredible, we were booked pretty much every Friday and Saturday night, we had a collection of videos from gigs and a digital camera full of ladies in pants, but most importantly, we never seemed to get tired or burned out? Which is something I really miss these days. Oh, and we finally got a pair of professional CD decks—a beautiful pair of Pioneer CDJ1000 MK2s. Life was sweet.

In 2007 I made another big decision and took the leap and moved from Clun to the big smoke of Shrewsbury, which I can tell you was a culture shock! I traded waking up to the sound of sheep and cows for heavy traffic and sirens. It really threw me off-piste and took me quite some time to adapt to it. I moved into a house with Rob, a lifelong friend of mine. We had been by each other's side since 1983, in playschool, primary school, and Secondary school. That's when I stopped holding his hand; he decided to be a bit more clever and wiser than me and got all educated up in university. Anyway, in 2007, he had just finished university, gaining some qualification in graphic design, and wanted to move to Shrewsbury but needed a housemate. He must have really missed me during his time at Uni because he was looking straight down the barrel at me for his new housemate. He asked me several times to move to Shrewsbury with him, but Clun and country life was my home, and it didn't appeal to me. Rob being Rob, though, wouldn't take no for an answer, and the idiot got me into the White Horse one Friday night, got me as p***ed as a parrot, and managed to sell the idea to me. Pratt.

The next day, very hungover and not knowing whether I was a man, a woman, or a lawnmower, he picked me up, and we went to have a look around a house in Shrewsbury. He obviously knew he would win me over, as he'd already found a place to look at before taking me to the pub. Following that brief visit, we went straight to the estate agent, who handed over a deposit to that house. I was a bit strapped for cash as usual, so he paid the deposit, plus he thought it was more of a sweetener. He just said I could pay him half back when I get another job, which was pretty much anyone's guess as to when that would be, to be honest. With that all signed and sealed, sobering up and realising that I was about to move house, all I needed to do then was break the news to my station officer at Clun and sort out a transfer from Clun fire station to Shrewsbury fire station, which unbelievably went seemingly well. It was a sad farewell to my fellow firefighter colleagues at Clun, but I was keen to get my sleeves rolled up in Shrewsbury.

By the time I had packed up my life in Clun and unpacked it in Shrewsbury with Rob, It was here that the Shrewsbury retained crew I joined could see I was a fish out of water in a town when we were out and about they would often ask me if I'd ever seen so much concrete and kindly gave me the nickname 'Combine', which was quite humorous.

The next important thing to do was to get a new job, which was something that wasn't too alien to me and came second nature. I wasted no time and set about getting my next career under my belt and did manage to get myself a job as a milkman about a week after we moved. Was this next job as a milkman going to be my new, much-loved career? Unfortunately not, I'm sad to report that after starting that employment on a Monday morning, by lunch time I had figured out it wasn't for me and called it a morning. I mean, driving a milk float, I was all for. I just didn't really take to getting all wrapped up like I was heading out on the piste working in a walk-in fridge sorting milk and yogurts. No sooner than my new boss had just finished drafting up my new contract, I was back in his office asking for my P45. So, with starting and ending employment all by lunchtime, by Monday afternoon, I was back at home job searching, and with that, I applied to be a postman, which I got. This was a brilliant job. I actually really enjoyed it; however, this somehow came with its minor complications.

2008, one year after living in Shrewsbury and still somehow employed as a postman despite turbulent employment by tearing the side out of a post van rendering it written off, getting bitten by a dog, getting locked inside someone's house who refused to let me leave because they thought I was a spy for the government and getting run over by a car for good measure, things on the DJ front were looking up so all wasn't too bad. It was the year I added another string to my DJ bow and got a regular gig in a nightclub called C:21 (now Havana Republic) in Abbey Foregate, Shrewsbury. This club was the crème de la crème, it was hugely popular, and people would queue up down the street to get into here at the weekend, including us; we always headed for C:21 at the weekend. This was a great move for me, and I loved it. I felt very lucky to be given a chance to DJ in this club. It was a stunning little quirky club that had larger than life décor, TV's all around the venue that played the music videos of the songs the DJ was playing, and another side club on the side of it called Spirit.

This was the first time I had ever DJ'ed a nightclub, and it was remarkably different from mobile gigs, mainly because it was a luxury just to walk in 10 minutes before my gig, play my set, then walk out with no strenuous setup or pack down to follow. I remember the only real difficulty I had to start was to DJ with DVDs. I was told I had to do this so the videos came up on the TV, so I had to get used to playing a music collection which wasn't mine which was a challenge, and it was also a little strange to DJ on my own for the first time without having Mark alongside me, especially if something went wrong! Which, in true fashion, it did a few times.

It wasn't too long, though, before I made friends at the club and acquired some new company, this is where I met fellow DJs Rob Mulliner and Colin Matty. Rob and Colin were the staple DJs in the club, and I'd step in when one wanted the weekend off or was unavailable. Eventually, Rob did three weekends out of four, and I then picked up the fourth weekend, which I always looked forward to. Colin was the resident DJ in Havana (C:21) in the main room, and I'd play the second room (Spirit). Although we did swap around a bit. I always used to go to the club at least an hour earlier to have a drink and catch up with Colin before my set. Sometimes though, we'd have a lot to catch up on and get talking for a little longer than we should have, but you always knew when you were over chatting as you'd catch the manager of the club standing somewhere where you couldn't miss him pointing to his watch, that was always my cue to get next door pronto and start laying down some bangers.

Now with a big vinyl backspin, let's go back a bit to 2005 before my move to Shrewsbury and before my great success as a milkman and postman. Something exceptional and hard to believe happened, which raised the bar for us, Mystikal Productions, we started working with the stars, and it looked like my dreams were beginning to come true as a young aspiring DJ.

Chapter 15
Shropshire and the stars

2005 was a major gear change for us as mobile DJs. The business was booming, we had a serious amount of equipment in the storage facility , and we were on the verge of having to ask mum and dad to move out of the house so we could have more storage. Mark was kept busy towing the trailer around from gig to gig in his Land Rover , and I was following close behind in my new upgraded posh transit van, which had four fewer rust patches on than the old one and a borderline pass on the MOT with only 20 advisories. Gigs were going to the next level, and we decided to introduce a video screen and projector to our rig, which proved to be a popular addition. On this, we could display music videos, graphics, and photos which went down extremely well with the public and really did make the whole set up stand out more and different from what any other mobile jock was offering at the time. But with all this, the rigs being expanded, and the introduction of the video screen meant more hands to deck. Mark and I started recruiting for more people to work with us on big gigs; that was easy, though, as we recruited some of our closest mates. They'd all graft hard for a few cold pints.

On our larger gigs, Mark and I were joined by Rob, our mate who I went on to live with in Shrewsbury. He was still in university at this point but would travel back at the weekend for beers and to help us out. Rob was at Cardiff university studying graphic design, which was very handy as he was a dab hand with graphics, websites, and a laptop. Rob did all our business cards and our website for us. On these large gigs, we employed him to take care of the visuals for the screen. Jon or Crangle, as he's known to many, my right-hand man, a hard grafter and likes the ale. Crangle was always with Mark and me propping up the bar in the White Horse on free weekends, seeing how many Strongbow and blacks he could drink before he won a mystery prize; it turns out he had to drink 8 pints of it one

Saturday night just to win me a Strongbow bottle opener, that's what you call a friend.

Crangle came on board and agreed to help us with driving and logistics and loved to get stuck into manual labour, providing he had a bottle of Mountain Dew to hand, Mountain Dew to him was like spinach to Popeye. He had a weird fascination with that. Crangle I had known for years, we first met in school back in 1995. To be honest with you, when I first met him, I thought he was a complete helmet, but I was wrong as I judged a book by its cover. He had to sit next to me in the school assembly; it was a 'Glad Rags' day where you wore your own clothes to school day for a quid. He walked up to his seat next to me clad in a Guns'n'Roses leather jacket, a pot of Bryl cream in his hair and a massive gold ear ring in his ear. I just stared, to be honest, in envy, I think; who knew that we would be the best of mates from that day on, and in later years, when we were in sixth form together, he helped me complete a G.N.V.Q. In business studies, I say helped. He did all the work and just printed off two copies of everything he did for me after changing a few words around, and in return I'd treat him to a battered beef burger and chips from the chippy at lunch time and a chocolate doughnut.

Rhys, a Prince among men, a gentle giant, a friend, and a fellow firefighter at the time at Clun fire station with me. Rhys would always be there when you needed him to lend a hand and had access to another van which was very handy; provided a cold beer was on the table, Rhys would go for gold. Good lad.

And last but not least, my former wingman, Lewis, DJ Ice himself, I was so happy to have him back on board for a gracious return. Although he was returning to a different roll this time, he swapped standing behind the decks to roaming the dance floor with a digital camera as our photographer taking snaps of the party people to upload on the big screen. I'm pleased to say that with him behind the camera, his photos contained no pictures of pants. Mark, by this time, though had no time for the digital camera as he was now too busy as the 'Lighting Jock' controlling all the lighting via mixing desks and computer-based software.

It was exactly like the Avengers Assemble, almost...well, nothing like it, but it felt like it to us. We had a brilliant team to help, and they all brought something to the table. Winners. So, with the expanded gigs all taken care of manpower-wise, we were ready to rise to the challenge of anything, and that we did.

I remember the call well. it was a Thursday night, and I'd just arrived home from drill night down at the fire station. I had a call from an organiser of events for a YFC club. He asked if we were available to DJ the annual Easter Ball they held, I was made up, this is one of the top three gigs we always wanted to play, and if that wasn't enough, they asked would we mind if we played alongside BBC Radio 1's JK and Joel. Wow, I nearly fell off my perch; talk about a double whammy there! JK and Joel, at the time were Radio 1's freshest new presenters, they did the early morning breakfast show and the Chart Show on Sunday afternoons, so they were extremely popular. It's no surprise I accepted without hesitation. I don't think I actually checked my diary either, but that didn't matter; this was a gig that I certainly wasn't going to pass on.

With that all signed and sealed, I immediately started the prep in my head, we were about five months or so off this gig, but I wasn't wasting no time. I was straight on the phone to Mark, then after, I thought, I really need the video screen and graphics for this one, so I was straight on the phone to Rob, not for long though as he was in Australia on his travels at the time, so I had to keep it short as to not run up a big phone bill and to not hold him up throwing copious amounts of alcohol down his neck for breakfast, I kept it to a minimum and in a nutshell just told him to make sure he was back, he could always pop back out to Australia after anyway. Easy as peas.

The venue the Easter ball was to be held in was the Ludlow Racecourse in Shropshire. It was being held in the large function room there. This is a fabulous venue for a gig; although there's no stage in there, there was portable staging. The room was separated by some bi-fold doors which could be opened to create more room. What was even better, though was they had a mass amount of TVs up high all around the room for people to watch when the races were on. That may not sound exciting to most, but that was exciting when you've got a technical genius on board who thinks they could re wire those TVs to share our graphics that we projected onto the big screen. It's the little things.

The Easter ball arrived, and it didn't disappoint; it was by far the best gig we had done to date. We had the full team on board with the expanded set up, and mum and dad actually got to see what their spare living room looked like again after we emptied it, I had all my music up to date and was excited to play all the latest bangers, meet and work with two BBC Radio 1 DJs and no doubt, in-between that, got on Mark's nerves for a change interfering with his lighting rig. Rhys and Crangle worked hard trucking diesel on the logistics, Lewis was primed with an empty SD card and a fully charged digital camera, and Rob was back from down under all set up with his array of posh laptops and graphics, and we even had an extra man on board that night, another Dan or 'Bungle' as he was known. He's a top man and assisted with the computer work. All was set up, and we were all ready for showtime. We were all done up and looking like the next big thing to come off Louis Walsh's production line, complete with our new matching business T-shirts. All we needed now was a couple of celebrities to arrive.

The boys arrived, looking far better than we did, we had matching T-shirts, and they had their posh leather jackets. Thinking back now, they had probably expected 'Champers' on arrival and traveling all the way from London, but instead, they were treated to a crate of non-chilled cans of Carling. Nevertheless, though, they polished those off and threw on a damn good party!

The night was massive,a huge success, the venue was at capacity, and the dance floor was packed from start to finish, everything went like clock work, and JK and Joel were great hosts and lovely people. We got on really well with them and, the following evening, went for drinks with them at another pub they were playing in Tenbury Wells, JK was from Tenbury originally, so when booked to come up this way, he killed two birds with one stone, so to speak and decided to play a gig in his home town the following evening which was a nice touch. That evening was also a little surreal for me as in one weekend, I had DJ'd with two BBC Radio 1 DJs and was having drinks with them behind the decks too. That was like a lottery win to me and was one step closer to feeling like that top DJ I'd set out to be.

All the hard work and effort we put into that gig led to us getting booked to play a further two more of these Easter balls in the following two years, which saw us again play alongside more BBC Radio 1 DJs to my delight. They came in the form of one part of Chris Moyles Breakfast Show team, Aled Haydn Jones, and future Radio 1 Breakfast Presenter and new kid on the block Greg James. All of these were also hugely successful events and propelled us into having no free weekends... ever!
Although there is one gig I want to mention that happened between working with Aled and Greg at the Easter balls; it was the night I was to DJ alongside my radio idol, BBC Radio 1's Scott Mills.

Chapter 16
Saturday Night Fever

Now 2006, and with our first celebrity gig under our belts with JK and Joel, we were buzzing for weeks after; what a giant leap forward and experience for us that was.

There was a void, though; we were left thinking, will we get another one of these Easter Balls? Will we work with radio royalty again? Who knew? We certainly didn't at the time. We were bouncing off one another and itching for more, then one night in the office with Mark, the White Horse pub's office. It came to me, why don't we host a celebrity gig ourselves? How hard can it be? So, with a dream idea in my head, six pints of Carling and a packet of prawn crackers in our bellies, and Mark tipsy enough to think I'd, for once, had a good idea. We made a start to find out how hard it actually was. We soon realised it was hard.

From the moment the idea came into my head, there was only one person I really wanted to work with - Scott Mills. There was no doubt about it, he was my radio Idol. I absolutely loved the man and still do. But he was the top of the tree as far as radio personalities went, so two things ran through my mind, how much would he cost, knowing he wouldn't come cheap, and could I get him from Radio 1 HQ in London to Shropshire??

We set to work. Obviously, this was a big challenge for us and a complete turn of tables as we always got booked for gigs, not organising them ourselves. We had no idea where to start with this. We fell on our feet here, though, as Rob was working for a graphic design company called SPA Creative, and Steve, who owned the business, was a tremendous chap. I got to know him when doing some work for him during my career breaks. Steve had a brilliant team working at the company. There was another guy, Big Rob; he was known as Lord Brockton. He was a creative man and really enthusiastic about most things you'd pitch to him. Rob knew about our idea of this gig, and Steve and Big Rob liked the idea also; they fully backed our thoughts and ideas so much that Steve said he'd financially back it. I can't remember if he was intoxicated at the time or not, but never the less this was amazing, we were so grateful to him and at the same time very excited as this gig was starting to get off the ground. We'd now got the financial backing we needed, so the next steps were to actually get a venue secured and fingers crossed... Scott Mills.

The venue we secured was the same venue we did the Easter ball at with JK and Joel, the Ludlow Race course. We chose this as it was a big venue, knew the layout, and after the JK and Joel gig, people would know it. Plus, as that Easter ball was a big success, we thought if we kept the venue the same, that would help things publicity-wise. With the venue secured, after a few weeks, the huge sound system from Dave was booked, the security, food, and bar were also in place, and we were nearly good to go. We Aptly named the event 'Mystik Fever'; clever work was done there. Not too sure where the fever bit came from. But that didn't matter.

Now, with all the above getting booked and secured, I had the job of getting Mr. Mills on board. I contacted his agency, and explained to them what we proposed; they then wanted it in a letter, so a letter was composed and sent to them, and a fee was agreed upon, great! He's coming then , is he? Not quite... "We have to give the letter to Scott to read and see if he accepts or rejects," they said. We will be back in touch in 24 hours to let you know. It was at this point I lost about four stone in weight in 24 hours, an absolute record, I'd imagine. I couldn't help but think we've got all this booked but may have to front it ourselves yet, we may have been Shropshire's superstar DJs in our minds, but I'm certain we wouldn't have drawn as much attention as Scott would have done to the punters.
Time seemed to have slowed right down on awaiting a reply from Scott's agency, whilst everything else was gathering speed, for that 24 hours, all the excitement for me completely stopped whilst I was holding my breath and getting stressed.

Finally though, after a good solid 24 -hour wait, a phone call from Scott's agency came, putting me out of my record weight loss attempt. "He's accepted," they said; I could not believe what I was hearing! Really? He's accepted? Wow, I said, that's fantastic news, and with that, all the legal bits were done, and I signed the contract. We officially had Scott Mills to headline our event. Now you may think I was being a bit daft worrying, but believe me, he could easily have said no. Thinking back, what I should have done was provisionally booked the venue first and then arranged the guest DJ, so I made things really difficult and risky for myself there. Standard practice.

Tickets were then designed and printed by Steve and his team, Rob created a temporary website to sell them on, and finally, like a track from DJ Jean, we were ready for the launch. Still, back in 2006, the likes of social media were thin on the ground and, I think, Bebo was just about the only social media platform out there, so we had to leaflet drop, poster everywhere and get word of mouth around and just never shut up about it, to be honest with you. We had to make this a success. Big Rob stepped in on the promotional side of this. He got the gig all over the papers and even secured an interview for us live on BBC Radio Shropshire to talk about the event, which was fantastic.

For the next few weeks leading up to the event, we tossed out all our CDs and cans of Lynx Africa and stuffed our glove boxes in the car and our pockets full of tickets and flyers for this event. We sold some and then a few more, but they weren't flying out of our pockets as we'd hoped for; not to worry, though, the websites were probably busier with sales. But on the website, the admin, or Rob should I say, could see how much traffic had been by the website and how many tickets had been sold. I went to the office only a few days before the event to check sales. If I'm honest, I wish I hadn't, this started me back off stressing again. Sales were slow and low. We needed, I think, 500 sales to sell out? Just a few days before the event, we'd sold around 80 to 100, which was abysmal; it was starting to become clear that we were heading for a financial disaster here, far quicker than a greyhound with its arse on fire.

Unfortunately, it got to the point where Steve had to call a serious meeting with us all and decide whether or not we pulled the event. It was close, very close, but I just wouldn't let it happen. I kept saying, it'll happen...it will, just you see! Everything moves a little slower in South Shropshire, and people will get them when they finish work on a Friday night. Well, that's what I hoped anyway, and that's what I prayed for the next few nights at least. I knew people would just turn up at the door too, but that was no good to rely on. I also kept saying how successful previous gigs at the racecourse were. They were sell outs, so its more than likely this one will be too. I think that was enough, just to keep them onside for now. After that meeting, for the next few nights, I prayed every night that we would wake up to a surge of sold tickets. It was at this point again my excitement for the gig had completely got up and gone, which was a real shame. It was an event working with my favourite DJ that I should be jumping for joy about, but being on the side of organising it this time, the stress put a dark cloud over it for me, temporarily of course.

So came the big day, I woke up nervous and stressed as usual. We loaded up all the gear and headed over to the Ludlow Racecourse to commence set up. We spent all day setting up, the expanded rig was looking superb, and Mark emerged out of the communication cupboard arse end first and covered in dust after we lost him in there a few hours earlier whilst he tapped into all the TVs up in the venue to show a live video feed. How does he know how to do these sorts of things? Mark was always like that, though. He was twenty-three dimensional in the way he'd see venues and always looked outside of the box before getting into one. In most venues we'd play, he would often disappear into a wall cavity or up in the ceiling hanging lighting and running cables to get that extra depth with lighting. Top man.

Anyway, with a sick feeling inside and feeling like I'd rather have a picnic in a mine field, a phone call came for a ticket and another then Mark's phone rang for tickets and Rob's phone too and they didn't stop ringing all bloody day! It was like a few drops of rain that started after months of drought and then turns into a storm. It came to a point where we had all downed tools and became call centre operatives. The website was crashing because of the traffic of people buying online too. We rang Jack at The White Horse, and he said that they had sold all their tickets too, and the tickets we had were burning holes in our pockets! I'm not kidding, hours this went on right up until the point of getting into the car to travel back to the venue to start. I was back at home trying to get tea sorted whilst selling tickets, the only time I took a break from selling tickets was when I had to take a shower, but after that, I was straight back on the phone selling tickets whilst standing in my pants trying to get dressed. By the time we had arrived back at Ludlow Racecourse, the team did a count-up of sales, and we'd done it; we had sold out, twice over, in fact! What an unbelievable turn around this was, and what a great success!

Let me tell you what a roller coaster of a few weeks leading up to this gig was. I can't remember when I'd ever been this stressed before, most probably the times I applied for a job and was required to show my CV. Knowing all tickets had sold and our finances were covered, the stress lifted, but then, like a smack in the face with a wet trout, the nerves came in. I could not win. Eight o'clock came, the stage was set, the doors opened to the people, and the show started. I was DJing the first hour or so, getting everyone warmed up. I remember feeling like I had a fully charged defibrillator strapped to my legs whilst all the nerves, anxiety and adrenaline soared through me. Along with trying to DJ feeling like that, I was also waiting for a phone call to say Scott had arrived. I was so glad when that call came so I could jump down off the stage and give myself a good shake. I remember getting off stage, walking through the doors behind me into another room. It was empty and quiet; all I could hear was just the noise of the bass coming from next door and a crowd of people getting all excited. I took a minute, took some deep breaths, jumped around, and ran around the room a few times before I walked outside to a posh car that was awaiting me there. I walked up to the car, grabbed a bag of CDs from the boot of the car, put my hand out, and warmly welcomed Scott Mills to Shropshire before finally shitting myself.

Luckily lady luck was on my side, and the aforementioned was just a figure of speech and didn't literally happen. We all got a great opportunity to have a chat with Scott backstage and grab some photos before he stepped up to the stage. I'll never forget the vibe and energy in that building when people started to see that we were preparing to introduce Scott, when anyone of us walked through the doors behind the stage, they could see Scott standing there, and the energy levels were pure electric. I left Scott in the company of the others whilst I kept on DJing, building the atmosphere to the max. Then it was time to bring Scott up to the decks; that moment was one I'd never forget, the crowd went crazy, and the noise certainly raised the roof. Once Scott started and he was settled, I took a moment to go outside for some fresh air and try to process everything we made happen. It was a phenomenal feeling, one of pure euphoria. We all, as a team, had managed to pull off a huge sell-out gig of our own with my idol Scott Mills fronting it. Unbelievable really. I'll always remember Crangle pulling me to the side and saying, "That's it, mate; you've done it now. You're definitely in," referring to me heading to be the top DJ I had always dreamed about. Had I made it? Was I in? Had I actually done it? I had absolutely no idea.

The night was a huge success; everything went to plan in the end. Although we were made up that the event was a sell-out, it was hard and sad to have to turn down people that turned up hoping to get in on the door. It turned out that at least another 200 people had arrived at the venue hoping to get in. Months of hard work and preparation went into that gig, from a simple idea with a pint to actually making it happen. So with that all completed, it was time to go back to the office, grab a pint and some prawn crackers and start again...not quite. We didn't get round to organising another gig of our own after this, well, we did have chats about the next one being with BBC Radio 1's Chapper's and Dave, but this was shelved no sooner it was mentioned. I can honestly say we just didn't get the time to start it all over again. We wanted to, but the work involved was insane, and we were constantly busy weekend after weekend DJing. I have the upmost respect for anyone that does that for a job, event organising, but thankfully, as mentioned before, we were lucky enough to DJ with more Radio 1 personalities at this venue, the Ludlow Racecourse but on these gigs, we didn't think and just jocked.

Chapter 17
Let's do some magic

If you can remember, way back, I mentioned that when I left school, in my record of achievement, I wanted to do three things with my life after education, be a firefighter, which I was doing, and be a DJ, which I think I was doing and the third job was to be a radio presenter.

2006, Here we go, who will have the brass to let me, this 'ooh arrr' Shropshire lad on the radio? Well let me tell you, a remarkable man did, and he is also another one of the best people I've ever met. His name was Austin, a man of impeccable talents, and he had a seriously impressive career spanning decades working with the best in the music business and record labels as well as being a professional radio presenter himself. As well as doing the DJing, I always had a burning passion for radio and was desperate to one day present my own show on the airwaves. It sounds so cliché, but I always imagined working for BBC Radio 1 in my bedroom when I was a nipper, doing the usual on a Sunday afternoon, sitting with a tape in my hi-fi listening to the chart show and trying to hit record on a song just at the right time the DJ stopped talking. I was certainly no different from any kid growing up in the '90s. I think that was just a right of passage back then. Once I'd got a tape full of music, when we went up to my nan's, I'd grab her keys to her Vauxhall Astra and sit in the car pretending I was on the radio with my tape of new hits.

I first met Austin back in, I think...1999 when I stepped through the doors of the local community radio station also in Newtown, Mid Wales, to do some school-based work experience. I stepped into Radio Maldwyn - The Magic 756 across mid-Wales and the borders 24 hours a day. It was brilliant! I'd have lived in that place. A real radio station. Good heavens. Radio Maldwyn was a lovely little place to be. It was a council-owned building situated at the back of the main car park in Newtown. It was a building that, despite having signs with Radio Maldwyn on the side of it, still confused some folk; on some days, it wouldn't have been an unusual sight to have someone walk through the doors into reception thinking it was a shop, it wasn't unusual for anyone to walk in just out of curiosity, and oddly enough, it didn't become an unusual thing for people to walk in thinking it was a public toilet either. This was comedy gold witnessing Austin being fronted by someone asking if its a toilet. I can't say I've ever walked into a public toilet with people sitting down at desks and having to be greeted at a reception area first.

Back in 1999, for work experience, I used to have to get a lift in to work with the salesman that worked at the radio station, Peter. Peter was a lovely, quiet man, although he did transform into something spectacular when on the way to work and on the way home. He loved his barbershop music and would put his tape on as soon as we got out of the built-up traffic area, then would sing like a tenor at the top of his voice all the way home, he was like the Go Compare guy off the tele. This was the first-time I'd ever been introduced to barbershop music and the last time I'd listened to it. My journeys to work were always interesting. In the daytime, it was Peter with his barbershop playing at maximum volume, and on the weekend, it was Dave with his clubber guide albums. Extremely diverse. I'd have loved to swap the music around.

Whilst on work experience there, I got involved with pretty much everything other than being on the radio. I went out with the sales team, watched how presenters compiled and presented their shows, had a good nose around the CD library, and I'm pretty certain I made my fair share of hot beverages too for everyone. I loved the place. Back to 2006 now, after several years away from Radio Maldwyn with copious amounts of gigs, joining the fire service and attempting to get to grips with employment. I decided it was time to make a serious effort with the radio business because, after all, I wasn't going to get my show on BBC Radio 1 without some form of experience was I, I was 24 years old and had grown out of sitting in my nan's car at the weekend pretending to present a show to the steering wheel, and Crangle thinks I'm heading there now after the Scott Mills gig so I'd best get a move on! I got in contact with Austin once more and asked if there was any work going on, paid or voluntary. Austin kindly took me in again and welcomed me back after several years away, but you'd be wrong in thinking I walked in there again and straight into broadcasting, no, this would never happen. In an age-old radio tradition, I was back in Radio Maldwyn as the tea boy. Yes, it's true; this is always the way you first make your mark in this industry and get your foot in the door, be good at making tea. The presenters would be on the air playing out song after song, and I'd be in the kitchen drumming with teaspoons with my head held high thinking, this time tomorrow, this could be me broadcasting over the airwaves of Mid Wales and beyond.

I'll always remember this, when I had my days off in the week, which I had quite often due to negotiations with alternative employment, I'd jump in my car and spend every bit of my free time (which I only had from Monday to Friday) at Radio Maldwyn. I'd be in the kitchen lining up the cups of tea, sat in the studios moithering the presenter, out in the foyer moithering Alan, the tech guy or mothering Austin about presenting a show. If there was someone to moither, I'd be moithering them. I worked my way around every part of that radio station, taking it all in and learning every part of the job that each and everyone played. Whether it be sitting with Alan watching him pre-program radio schedules and do 'com prod' (commercial production) or sitting with radio presenters in the studio, live on air, watching them with a keen eye on how they did it. When I wasn't doing that, I'd be sat with a presenter in another room and watch them produce their next show, then when I wasn't doing that and felt brave enough, I'd go and sit in the production studio where Martin, who worked in sales at this time and a former presenter would be voicing commercials and quite often, when he went wrong, would educate you with every single profanity known to man, there was millions of them. Martin was brilliant, one of the nicest people you could meet, however, he had a very short fuse and could enter a state of rage in about two seconds flat from being calm. Naughty Martin. You wouldn't believe a man could practically pass out due to rage from voicing a bird seed advert. That's another memory that will stay with me forever.

Mainly though, Austin was my target, the man that would see me most, with my continuous presence hanging around, itching to broadcast. Patience is a virtue, though, as they say, and the day finally came where, after Martin had finished his commercial recordings in the second studio, effing and blinding about bird seed and cornflakes, Austin would make me go in there and practise my presenting techniques, which was difficult because, after all those years talking to a steering wheel thinking I was good, it turned out I actually had none. Alan would get it all switched on with a dummy show, and I'd sit in there for hours learning how to use the equipment and the mixing desk whilst it was all recorded-on minidisc for Austin to listen back to. I took up an awful lot of his time listening to me waffle on about what was going on outside despite making it up as there weren't any windows in there or how I was nearly late and how the morning had been a rush, which was tempting fate as you'll read later on. I was making anything up in my links just to make it sound like a normal show. I certainly would never listen to them ever again, given the chance. I'd finish recording a demo and leave the studio, and Austin would walk in to listen. Thirty seconds later, he'd walk back out and tell me to go back in. I did find this quite entertaining and exciting, though. It was like a game show, which demo was going to strike gold, if any.

It's funny what you think you know, and then, in reality, you don't. I thought I could do a radio show with ease, but how wrong was I. There was so much to learn in the art of broadcasting that you'd never ever think of, but after months of coaching and pointers from Austin and the other presenters, the day came when I was successful in my latest attempt. I walked out of the studio, and Austin walked into the studio. I knew I was onto a winner with that last effort as he lasted over a minute in there this time. He came out and gave me a thumbs up, and said to me, "Good effort, kid". Finally, I'd made some progress. The trouble I had was I'd talk far too fast and try to cram all I had to say into a single link very quickly. If I was to pull out, the best piece of advice Austin ever gave me that stuck and seemed to work was when he told me to slow down and imagine your just talking to a mate in the pub. Anything that involved the pub was always a good thing to me, and it worked in a roundabout way on radio too. Just a few years ago now, when I popped the question to my wife, I was talking to Austin about my proposal and said I hadn't been that nervous since he used to make me do those demo show. I'll always remember his reply, he said, "Well, you've done two things right in your life now" I loved that.

Right, with Austin giving me the thumbs up on the demo, it was from that moment onward big things were coming my way, Austin confirmed he was going to put me on air, and I was officially going live on air across Mid Wales and the borders as 'the weather kid'. That's right, on the hour every hour, you'd hear my voice delivering you the weather, I'd be with you wherever you were come rain, wind or shine. The best job in the world this was, I'd hit the jackpot. I was so proud of myself, and so was my dad; Primrose did good. I had a feeling that I was becoming part of the furniture at Radio Maldwyn because I noticed one day I was given my own pigeonhole. If you're old enough to know what that is. If not, then all it was was a little space in a shelf with my name on it where all my letters and CDs went and sometimes a ridiculously strong Belgian beer from another presenter, Mike Baker, when I had done some work for him or covered his show whilst he took off for a weekend sampling different beers in Belgium.

Each weekend I'd be at the radio station doing my weather broadcasting on the hour, and then for the rest of the hour, I'd be sat in the studio monitoring the show that was going out on the air on Sunday afternoons you see, the station like many others would play a pre-recorded show by a presenter, and it was my job on a Sunday to sit there, in the studio making sure it ran smoothly and to pause it when ad breaks needed to be played and resume it afterward until on the hour the news would play followed by my 30 seconds of air time. I can understand that this doesn't sound all that appealing, but for someone who was obsessed with radio like I was, it was brilliant, and I knew that I wasn't in a position to turn my nose up at any job going if I wanted to progress.

Eventually, after sitting in on Sundays doing this shift for several months, things did progress, and I was given the opportunity to present a live show on a Sunday morning. This was a golden opportunity that I'd been waiting for for a long time. Finally, it was my time to fill with more than just what the weather was doing. I was absolutely thrilled with this opportunity, and I couldn't afford to mess this up. Seven o'clock on a Sunday morning; a young DJ in his early 20s, making the most of a Saturday night—
what could possibly go wrong? Bloody plenty, that's what.

Chapter 18
The Prince of Dead Air

So, finally, I had been given my big break on the radio, to present a new three-hour show at seven on Sunday mornings with my debut show imminent. The world was informed about my debut, and many friends and family were excited to tune in and see what I had to offer on a Sunday morning other than just the weather forecast. I do remember Alan had mixed up all my show idents which I was so excited to hear, Idents being the little 10 seconds sweepers that play on radio shows saying who's now on or what radio station you're listening to, etc. They were excellent; I had a preview of these before the debut show, although one particular ident took me straight back to the early DJ days when we were playing about with names to label ourselves with. This particular ident was played, and it went something like, "Dan Morris...The Clun Valley Kid on Radio Maldwyn The Magic 756." Well, I wasn't expecting that to drop in. Straight away, I just imaging myself rolling up to the studios saddled up on horseback with a couple of pistols by my side, looking very much like the Milky Bar Kid but shouting,]The Music is on me!' whilst everyone in the car park cheered on in sheer delight. I wasn't quite sure how to take it, but me always favouring comedy and never taking myself seriously went with it, plus, I would have never been able to ask them to remove it after all they have done for me.

Here we go, then. I think it's about time things hit the fan once more. It was 2006, I believe, World Cup time, I seem to recall. My mate, Rob, held a big all-day party up at his dad's farm. We had barn all kitted out with our large video screen, and Mark, in all his glory, didn't let us down. He had sweet-talked his folks to stick to watching free view TV for the weekend as he had taken a ladder to the side of their house and took the sky satellite dish down, complete with the sky box to get that all set up on a large scaffold pole in a field to broadcast the football in the barn complete with our speakers hooked up to it all. It was impressive, to say the least. We had a big gathering there with drinks plenty and as much BBQ food as you could eat, it was a very hot summer's day too, I remember, so everything was bob on perfect.

Unfortunately, I couldn't partake in the drinking activities that day because it was my debut show on Radio Maldwyn the following morning at seven, so I had to be sensible, and sensible I was too, probably for the first time in my life. I'd deliberately driven up to Rob's party, so I had the car there and had to stay sober. Things were going well; the sun was shining, all my mates were all together, we (they) were drinking, eating, having a kick around in the field, just loving life on a beautiful summers day in Shropshire, having a good laugh, although, the trouble was when you start to see everyone else getting into the party spirit as the day drew towards the evening and you've hit your quota of shandy because your the only one left driving. We all know that can be tough at the best of times unless you have superior willpower, which, unfortunately, I was never blessed with.

As I said, all was going well until some tosser who shall remain nameless piped up and said there was a barn dance on over in Wales that night; after a day of football, BBQ, and drinks, all my mates that were there thought the barn dance just over the border in Wales would be the perfect end to the day, and I agree...if you weren't staying sober and having an early start the next day. Being close-knit to the YFC, I did know that this barn dance was on, but I kept quiet about it all day as I knew that everyone would take off there that evening, and I'd be left to head home to get an early night, but as soon as that individual piped up and let the cat out of the bag about the barn dance, all attention turned to that. Bugger. For the next few hours, I did do my very best to convince everyone that the barn dance would be total crap, but they didn't listen, and It wasn't long before everyone at the party had decided they were going to head over to this dance anyway, everyone except me who had to...well...reluctantly say no. What a bore. This was extremely tough to turn down as everyone else was going, but I had no choice but to be the sad act to go home...or was I?

Crangle, being the mate he was, was concerned about me and didn't want me to be left out. He was trying to encourage me to come over and not drink, that was a big ask, and I knew my willpower would never work with that. I declined. But Crangle wouldn't give up; he's like a Jack Russell dog chasing a yoghurt pot around the front room. When he gets going, he won't stop. Don't get me wrong, I was tempted, and cracks were appearing; Crangle could see this as he knew me too well. Then, eventually, after all his persistence, the most idiotic, most ridiculous, stupid thing happened on my part. I put a deal across to him. I said that I'd come to the barn dance with him and the others, and in return, he's got to be up early on Sunday morning and come with me to the radio station for my first show at seven, which meant getting up at 5:30 a.m. and leaving at 6:00 a.m. No surprise, Crangle agreed to the deal; after all, he did eat a bar of soap in school when I dared him to, so if you agree to eat soap, let's be honest, there's not much you wouldn't agree to, is there?. So, with that stupid deal done, the car was taken back to my house, and my lift to the barn dance picked me up en route; this, you can see, was a recipe for disaster slowly unfolding.

We descended down the narrow roads into wonderful Wales, through the valleys, and down some tracks until we were met with droves of people headed towards a large cow shed in a field lit up and vibrating with music. These dances were brilliant; some large dusty cow shed during the week full of manure was transformed into a pop-up nightclub. We DJed many of these barn dances mainly for the Shropshire YFC, so it was nice to actually frequent one as a night off over in Wales. We passed through the horsebox trailer, where you paid your entry fee and got your wristband. You then entered the vast building, where immediately you'd head over to a load of upturned potato boxes with black hay bale wrap stapled to them, doubling up as a makeshift bar. There you'd hand over a couple of quid for the best warm can of Carling or Strongbow you'd ever tasted. If you were lucky, you may have had a cold one if they had fridges there. But this was a barn dance; you didn't care. They were just too good to worry about the temperature of your beer; you'd only have a few of those anyway before one of your mates came back with a handful of unknown shots that tasted like acetone and sheep dip, which then left a feeling of fire in your mouth so a warm can actually felt cooler then.

We were having a great time at this barn dance; drinks were flowing, and music was playing. We, the boys, were all together, and each shot we had made us smell more and more like a hospital. As the evening went on, my concept of time had gone out the window, and all my willpower too! However, believe it or not, I still didn't drink all that much; well, at least, I didn't think I had. I wasn't using my head to prop me up at the toilet, which usually indicates how much I've consumed; no, I was still conscious about my debut radio show at 7:00 a.m. the next day. Time check, please. Gone three in the morning now, bloody hell. Crangle and I have just walked through the door back home. Crangle and I are both singing our favourite song from Ghostbusters 2, swaying all over the place with a ravenous appetite for frankfurter sausages with plastic cheese and a packet of Pom Bears. Perhaps I did have a little more than I thought! After that nutritious late-night feed, we headed to bed to get some sleep as in three hours' time, it was show time. Knobs.

My eyes opened, daylight bursting through the small gap in the curtains. I felt tired, slightly hungover, and the moment I thought about my first show, the nerves and adrenaline kicked in. I was happy I was awake in good time and was happy and very surprised that I'd woken up before my alarm went off; however, that feeling of happiness was short-lived and about to come to a very abrupt end. The thing is, my alarm didn't go off and was never going to go off because I didn't set an alarm. I looked at the time, and it was the most horrific thing I'd seen in my life, far, far worse than the first time I'd watched Jaws as a child, where Quint falls into the shark. The time was 8:30 a.m., and I was meant to have been live on the air at seven!!! Which meant I should have left home at six! Hells teeth, I was up the creek now. I launched myself out of bed, gently slapped Crangle very hard on the head, and told him to quickly move his arse and bloody quickly!!! He hadn't got a clue what was going on. He was all over the place. We didn't have time for anything other than to get changed, get in the car, and get to the radio station bloody pronto.

On the way there, I put the radio station on, to my horror, and what I didn't want to hear was nothing. Unluckily for me, though, I and everyone tuned into Radio Maldwyn this Sunday morning to listen to the Clun Valley Kid being spoiled with a great big nothing, nada! Absolutely nothing was being broadcast, and this is what they call dead air in the industry, and it's an awful thing to have on any radio station; every second of dead air feels like an hour, and that was the longest hours drive to the radio station, to anywhere at that matter I've ever had. "I've completely and utterly cocked this up now!" I shouted to Crangle, who had one foot in the grave next to me. I was mortified and so disappointed with myself for this. Then, about 10mins away from arriving at the radio station, the radio came back to life, and music began to play. Although this, you'd imagine, was a great thing, and it was for the listeners, it also meant that someone knew that there was a problem and had to go and fix it. Alan, the station's technical guy, that's who.

We finally arrived and burst through the station doors looking like we'd just washed up on shore and stunk like the chlorine foot tray at swimming baths. I left Crangle to collapse at reception and ran to the studio; Alan was sat there. He didn't say much but just had a grin on his face whilst no doubt thinking to himself, tit. Alan, I didn't fear too much; it was Austin that I was fearing. In the studio, there was a little red phone on the side that was exactly like the presidents have in the films, it was the bat phone, this was the important phone that only really really important phone calls came in on in an emergency, and when it rang, it would ring silently with just a little strobe light flashing on it, and it was this phone on this particular day, I did not want to see ringing. Only two people had the number to that phone; Alan was one, and Austin was the other.

So, marginally late, the show went on, and I actually did my job of presenting my first show, which wasn't exactly how I planned it to go. I was starting to wake up and calm down, whilst my mate was to the side of me; looked like he could have done with being hooked up to a drip. Things were all good, and order had been restored across the airwaves, but one thing was lurking at the back of my mind, had I gotten away with this slight early morning mishap? I was starting to think I had until stone me that red phone started flashing at me. As my whole body stiffened up and my trousers started squeaking, I picked up the phone with a shaking hand to a gentle, subtle voice: "Hi, mate, you, okay?" It was Austin. He was calm; he wasn't angry or mad. And he asked me how the show was going. Confused was an understatement; I thought he was going to fire me instantly after I'd finished the show, but he didn't. It was then I thought I'd definitely gotten away with it, and just as we were finishing up our conversation, he proceeded to say, "Oh, and next time, get a bloody clock that works, and don't present me with dead air again." And with that, the phone went down, and I well and truly ripped the stitching in those trousers of mine.

Somehow and to this day, I still don't know how. Call it a miracle, but for once, I wasn't fired. You could have gotten fired for doing far less than that, I almost wanted to fire myself for Austin, but I kept my job, and Austin kindly gave me a second chance to redeem myself. Which I was forever grateful for, but it will come as no great surprise that I was never to broadcast at 7: a.m., especially on a Sunday again anytime soon. I did, though, keep my nose clean with Austin and Radio Maldwyn from that day on, I only relapsed once as far as I can remember, and that was because a supermarket sponsor advert made me cross because I'd forgotten to play it several times between the news and the weather on the hour every hour and resulted in me firing off an expletive. This only came to light because Austin casually opened the door of the studio I was broadcasting from and said to me,

"kid, next time you feel the need to say Bollocks, can you make sure you've got the mic off and don't actually broadcast it on air? You may like the word as I do, but many don't and may find it offensive."

Austin didn't miss a trick. He was always listening and always had a presence. With that small, brief matter swiftly taken care of in a true Austin dress down, I continued my path in radio. I went on to host my own evening shows, which were better time suited for a young DJ on Friday and Saturday nights on Radio Maldwyn called 'DM in the PM', which were great fun, quite often I'd do the radio show, and then go and DJ at a gig straight after, it was a busy and chaotic lifestyle at the weekend, but I loved it. As well as having my own shows, I'd often sit in for other presenters on their shows when they had holiday leave, and I even did the live Christmas morning shows too. I was trusted with time by then and had matured some. In my time there, I had presented the breakfast show, mid-morning show, the afternoon show, and evening and weekend shows, so basically broadcast over every hour really.

I worked happily with my radio family until November 2010, when, unfortunately, due to the times, Radio Maldwyn hit financial problems and went into administration. This was devastating for me and the others that worked there; such a sad time. Unfortunately, I had to accept that my time at Radio Maldwyn The Magic 756 was done. I remember that day like it was yesterday. It felt like a sledgehammer taking us all down. It was just a normal day until some big coats walked through the door. Austin called us all into the reception area, where these big coats stood behind him. He then delivered the bad news. As far as I'm aware, the shows stopped with immediate effect, and the station was just left to play non-stop continuous music from there on in. It wasn't long before the phones all lit up with concern from listeners wondering what was going on. After scratching our heads for some time and trying to come to terms with what just happened, we wandered around and started doing a horrible thing, grabbed some boxes, and started packing up our possessions and life at Radio Maldwyn. It was over.

I still to this day still talk about my time served at Radio Maldwyn with people, and the easiest way of describing it and a way to get a feel for how it was for me there is to watch a film called 'The Boat That Rocked'. That pretty much hits the nail on the head for how it was for me, minus a few things obviously and that we weren't on a boat, we were firmly anchored up at the back of a pay and display car park in Mid Wales. Radio Maldwyn ceased in November 2010 and, around 12 months later, was bought by another company and relaunched as Radio Hafren. None of the original presenters returned. A few years later, Radio Hafren also ran into complications and also closed down. This was the last time the building was to ever be a radio station, and the community of Mid Wales and the borders were left to re-tune their radios for good. The building was gutted from all the broadcasting equipment and later became a charity shop before being demolished. On the original site of Radio Maldwyn now stands a grand new visitor centre called Hafan Yr Afon, and at the time of writing this, this is to be where Ashley Owen, another former Radio Maldwyn presenter, is organising a Radio Maldwyn reunion on the 1st July 2023 to mark 30 years of when Radio Maldwyn started, at 7:56 a.m. on the 1st July 1993.

After the demise of Radio Maldwyn, the radio work didn't stop there; I was very fortunate. With all the experience I'd gained from Radio Maldwyn had created a healthy looking Radio CV, which was far superior and more important than my normal working CV. Over the next few years, I was lucky enough to get several more radio gigs. Obviously, I was still sending demos to the programme controller at BBC Radio 1 regularly, which didn't amount to anything, sadly, so I continued to focus on commercial and community stations up and down the country. I first got involved with an internet-based radio station, to begin with after I left Radio Maldwyn called Pipeline Radio, where I hosted a weekly dance show which was available as a podcast each week on iTunes, which was brilliant and the first time I could really base a show on the music I enjoyed at the time.

I got a gig on a radio station based in Alicante, Spain, called Heat FM, a classic club show which, again, was brilliant fun to host and was great fun to play all the classics. I did this show from my own personal studio I put together in the spare room at my house; I'd record the show each week and then send it over to Kev in Spain, who would then load it into the station's play-out system to be broadcast.

I then, through Austin, got in and on WCR FM (Wolverhampton City Radio) and presented a show called 'Now That's What I Call a Radio Show', which was broadcast every Sunday and showcased the 'Now' compilations, a big thanks to Andy Walters for that opportunity. This show was a little different from what I was then doing with all the dance music, but I really enjoyed it because I had the full collection of the Now albums; there was no end to memories I could create.

But before I went to WCR FM and Heat FM....there was a wonderful radio station broadcasting from the magnificent Isle of Man called Energy FM.

Chapter 19
The Isle of Dan

With the doors at Radio Maldwyn now firmly shut and with dead air once again playing out over the frequency, which this time wasn't my fault, I was left without full-time work but more painfully out of work within the radio industry, which I loved. What was I going to do now?

I was still working in the fire service as a firefighter, and Mark and I were still busy with Mystikal Productions doing gigs most weekends, but I now needed a full-time job once more and more preferably one in radio again too, which I knew wasn't going to be easy. December 2010 was very bleak for me, out of work, out of radio, and not earning barely enough to get by on, my rented house was put up for sale, so I had to move out into a small flat with no heating at winter time, I lost £2k due to a bad investment, and I had to sell my car to make ends meet. It was a dreadful time. I had practically lost everything. The only money I had coming in was from the fire service but with no other income, that would only just cover my rent at the time. The money from the gigs we did just went into investing in more equipment which was crazy looking back now, I really needed some of that.

Myself, Austin, and the rest of the guys from the radio station regularly met up on socials though which was a break from the bleakness and kept my mental health in check. The guys would jump on a train on a Saturday, and we would all meet up for the afternoon in Shrewsbury to have a good catch-up with some food and beer. We were all in the same boat though, all throwing in demo tapes to every radio station in the country just hoping one would bite. By 2011 I had got the gig on Pipeline Radio, which was great, but this was voluntary and for the love of the job only. I needed paid work, as Austin would say, a real job. I did get myself on to a working agency for non-radio work, and they got me some work in a parcel warehouse. I wasn't a fan of this, but I desperately needed the money. Once that contract was up, I was moved to sorting mail again for another company before then moving on to become a courier, which I was offered full-time. At least now I was financially safe and could continue to seek out radio work whilst the bills were getting paid. I still wouldn't settle for non-radio work.

Austin had many contacts in the radio industry and put me in contact with a man called Juan. Austin had hired Juan and gave him that break on radio many years ago, just like Austin did with me at Radio Maldwyn. Austin said it had been many years since he had last spoken with Juan but told me to get in touch with him as he now runs his own successful radio station and mention Austin's name. I did this straight away, thinking nothing would come of it, but after a demo was sent to Juan, he came back interested and wanted to hire me as Mid-Morning presenter on a station called Energy FM of, which he now owns, it was fantastic news, I'd finally landed back on my feet and got a job in full-time radio again. My only worry was it was in the Isle of Man.

I only worried it was in the Isle of Man because it was a long way away and meant I'd have to relocate, It felt even further away because it was overseas. Not exactly the other side of the world by saying overseas but being a non-traveller, that bit of water between Liverpool and the Isle of Man made it feel trans-Atlantic to me. I only moved from the village of Clun to Shrewsbury in 2007, which was only 39 odd miles apart with a friend. How was I going to manage to go further afield on my lonesome? My one advantage now was that, I could tell the time. We were now in March 2011; I'm back in paid work by only a few months with a new job and was starting to get myself stable again; what should I do? I was extremely confused. I wanted the job desperately but relocating overseas, albeit a short hop across the Irish sea was a million miles out of my comfort zone on a monumental scale. Although I was back in employment and earning again, which would have kept me secure and stable financially, me being me didn't give that a second thought because radio was calling again. I'll give Mark a call, he will be able to talk some sense, luckily, it was a call well worth having, he was encouraging and sympathetic when I spoke to him about it, all he said was, "Just get on the boat." Really useful that was; I don't know why I worried. After Marks extremely comforting one to one, I then thought I'd get a second opinion of what I should do and sent Austin a lengthy email too, asking him an array of questions, his answers weren't much better than Marks to be honest, although they were far more brutal and downright hilarious which still to this day has me in tears when I read back on that email I still have, I would have loved to copy and paste that exact email in this book, but unfortunately, and I have tried, I'm unable to even edit them to make them somewhat suitable which is a shame. After reading it over and over again until I stopped laughing, I gathered that he wanted me to accept it and that it would be a good move. Austin used to live in the Isle Of Man and did radio many years ago over there long before Radio Maldwyn, so he was clued up with what the island offered.

So, after much thought and deliberation, I accepted the contract and the job, and now I had to sort everything else out. I handed in my notice at my relatively new job; this was the easiest thing to do on my list as it was something that I was used to, well, I usually just disappeared from my employer and went AWOL, but this time, I was a little more formal with it and actually let them know I was off. I then had to speak to the fire service, who kindly gave me a six-month sabbatical. I handed in my notice on my rented flat, put all my bits and pieces into storage, and gave my cat and washing machine to Mum. The only thing I had left was one suitcase which I was taking with me, which was crammed tighter than my dad's wallet. Now, there's almost a little bit of history repeating here; I was all set for the off; I was leaving on a Sunday in June, June 5th to be precise, the day before Marks birthday and three days before mine, but Rob was getting married in the July of 2011 and had his stag doo on the Saturday night before I flew off to the Isle of Man, luckily though, I didn't miss anything this time, especially my flight, I'd learnt from my mistakes, but it did cause extra stress and a little fear I must admit. I did, however though, take another hangover with me, which wasn't pleasant.

I remember that departure day well; Rob took me to

Birmingham airport and waved me goodbye on my travels, but he didn't go home empty-handed; no, I didn't get him a nice leaving gift; he went back home with half the contents of my suitcase I took with me, he went back with a mixture of my shoes, pants, socks, jeans and anything else I could spare out of the suitcase as it was too heavy, and they wouldn't let me through to board unless I got the correct weight. I was beginning to think that I was the genetic son of Frank Spencer. This was ridiculously embarrassing doing this in full view of the people in the lines checking in, and it was something that didn't help my stress levels one bit, I'd have been happy to just have just collapsed, to be honest with you, and wake up back at home and it have been all a dream. I'm surprised I didn't just give up there and then get back in the car with Rob and go home for a burger and a pint at spoons. Any other job that included me having to give my mate my pants, I'd have just quit. I wouldn't have thought twice, so that, I guess, will give you an idea of how much I loved radio. With the airport fiasco all sorted and finally being allowed to board my flight, I was off on my global, trans-Atlantic flight of 40 minutes to the Isle of Man, or the 'Isle of Dan' as the lads had so aptly titled it.

The Isle of Man is a beautiful place to be. Such a stunning little island, I'd never seen anything like it before. The scenery of the island certainly helped. I felt like a fish out of water, pushed far beyond my comfort zone, and had no family or friends to lean on. This was the ultimate test for me. I really was a stranger on the shore. I met some brilliant people there and loved the job I was doing; I was insane, though, as I was still taking gigs as per normal on the mainland back home and spending my time and money flying backwards and forward all the time to do them, this was a very fast-paced life and kind of crazy now when I think about it.

After my 40-minute journey, I successfully navigated my way off the plane and through to the arrivals part at the Ronaldsway airport and was collected by a nice man called Mark. I did think, how the hell am I going to know who to look for when I get there, He'd spot me straight away, Frank Spencer coming through the arrivals. It didn't take me long to see him, though, as he was holding one of those boards with my name on it. It was a large board with Energy FM at the top of it and my name underneath it; bloody posh that was. Once we had thrown my half suitcase in his car, he then drove me to my new boss, Juan's house where he kindly gave me a room and a car. By now, I was falling apart inside, the nerves had shaken me to near collapse, I've packed up my life in Shrewsbury, gave my mate my pants at Birmingham Airport, and flown for the first time on my own to a place I'd never been to, to then live in a house with my new boss who I'd never met, to then do a live radio show the next day having never set foot in the building, seen or used the studio equipment and not knowing the format of my new radio show. Now that's some love for radio, is it not? I was torturing myself going out of my comfort zone that far, although, as bad as it felt at the time, I did question myself. Why was I doing this? I have no regrets about doing so. I believe it's good to get out of your comfort zone and do something new occasionally. I strongly believe that's how you can grow. But maybe try a little push before a leap like that. I was a walking wreck.

On Monday morning, I woke up in my new life and was immediately shaken with fear again. I don't think there were many mornings in my life where I ever woke up relaxed and calm. I was always waking up with some form of stress or anxiety. I remember the first thing I did was text Mark happy birthday and apologised for being unable to have a pint with him. After that, pure panic kicked in as I was due to go live on air at 7:00 a.m. Juan drove me to the radio station and gave me a pair of headphones and a crash course on how the playout system worked. My only comfort at this point was that the mixing desk was exactly the same as what I was used to at Radio Maldwyn, so that was literally the only thing I could steer. Seven o'clock arrived, and it was show time; I felt so sick, but I had no option. I had to open up the mic and go live. It was a three-hour show I had, and I can say that those three hours were the quickest of my life but certainly not smooth. Another presenter at Energy, Stefan, kindly sat in with me on my first show just in case I struggled with operating anything, to which I did, most of it, but he was a god send sat there with me and became my new best friend instantly. After finishing my show, I was taken off to the TT races to witness that firsthand, which was incredible. I'd never been into motorsports, but seeing that firsthand soon did.

I soon settled in and had no choice after being thrown into the deep end like that. I soon found my feet again. I started to settle into the radio station, got to know the brilliant staff that worked there, and found my own style with my mid-morning breakfast show, which I presented. On weekends when I wasn't working and wasn't back home on the mainland, I'd often jump in the car and go off exploring the island. Mark was a top mate while I was away in the Isle of Man. He came over to visit me on a couple of occasions which was nice of him. He came over one weekend with another best friend of mine, Pete. Both Pete and Mark came over on the weekend in August to a music festival that was on, Mannifest 2011. It was so good to see them both, and it was a huge comfort.

I'll always remember one Saturday I was doing a Saturday morning show on Energy FM, and a staff member came into the studio and said I had a visitor. This confused me as I wasn't expecting anyone and more to the point, I didn't know anyone either! Who on earth has come to visit me? I said to send them in, and would you believe it? Mark walked through the doors! Unbelievable! I think this was the happiest I'd ever been to see him! Totally surprised me he did. He didn't even let me know he was coming over, mind you. If I didn't return home when I did, after another mishap with a gig that was to follow, I don't think he'd have ever come to visit me again. You wouldn't believe it, but another clanger was just up ahead on the horizon for us.

Chapter 20
Mark Went to the Moon

Now, as a DJ, I was used to 'flying solo' performances with DJ gigs in the club when Mark wasn't available; however, it was now Mark's turn to feel what working solo felt like, unfortunately, though it's not quite the same when you're doing a mobile gig, and you're not the DJ, which awkwardly he was about to experience what that felt like first-hand but not by choice. For many years we did an annual YFC gig called the Purslow Show Dance, which was our first regular big gig if you like. It was held in a large marquee in a field just down the road from another cracking pub called The Hundred House Inn in a place called Purlsow which was around four miles away from the village of Clun. It was one we always looked forward to doing every year, and we did them year after year without fail. This year's '2011' Purslow Show Dance was going to be a little different, though, missing a DJ and featuring one irate lighting jock.

It's nearing the end of August 2011, and I'm still on the radio doing the mid-morning show in the Isle of Man; as I said before, we still took gigs as normal, and nothing changed there. August was the month of the Purslow Show Dance , and we were booked again to play there. It was about a week to go before the gig, and the usual prep began with a phone call to Dave Cornish for the large sound system and a, by now, a nice new van hired as the other van had turned its 20 advisores into 20 critical failures and retired into a skip on Dad's driveway which I didn't miss as it looked horrendous by now. I don't think the garage even bothered to attempt the MOT; they just said it's a write-off. This year though, there was the added extra of booking a flight back.

I remember I came off air after my show finished, and the first thing to do was book my flight back for the gig. I was speaking to my boss, Juan, before I booked the flights, in general conversation Juan then said to me, don't forget there's a live broadcast that I was involved with happening next Saturday, which I need to be at. "Oh, dear," I muttered to myself; he was talking about the same Saturday that I had to get back to for the gig. I explained that I needed to get back for the gig I had booked in. However, it was my fault, and I had genuinely forgotten about this broadcast that was happening. This was an important live broadcast, and he didn't have anyone to step in and cover for me, Juan wouldn't budge on this, no matter how many times I told him the world would end if I didn't make it back for the gig. Juan was a great boss and was very flexible with me, but on this particular date , he simply said that I was required to work there at the live outside broadcast, which was that which, as it was my job, I couldn't really argue the matter.

After our discussion, I calmly walked over to my desk and sat down. Bloody hell fire, what was I going to do now, then? I can't cancel the gig for two reasons one, it's too short notice, and I can't let them down, and two, if I did cancel it and they got someone else in to do the gig, we'd never do the gig again, that's how the system generally worked if you turned down a gig you were offered, rarely would you get asked again to do it the following year and I couldn't afford to let that happen.

I needed to call in the A-team to save this, and I needed to have a very sensitive conversation with Mark too; the thought of having to call him and explain what was happening on this side of the water and what I needed him to do to save this gig was about as pleasant as the thought of putting your testicles in a red hot vice and my track record of so-called important calls to Mark weren't very good. Anyway, I had no doubt whatsoever that this conversation was going to send him cheaply into orbit. Naturally, I called the other lads first and explained the predicament I had created, they found it quite funny, and each of them found it even more comical when I told them that I'd got to ask Mark to DJ it, down to the fact that he was going to go full on ape shit with me.

After much pacing and deliberation, and not able to hold off any longer I called Mark and explained everything openly and honestly to him and how there really was one way of doing this gig, and it is with no great surprise he wasn't best pleased at all after he had done a 360 of Jupiter and returned to earth, he again surprised me with how much bad language there was in the world, which I can't blame him for. Most of it was covered, Mark would see to the speaker collection, Rhys would help with the setup, and Crangle would collect the van and help with the setup, etc. The only thing that was missing was a DJ as he was stranded on an island out in the Irish sea, which is an issue and, oddly enough, a vital part of the machine. There was only one person now who could do the DJing.

Mark, don't be silly; you can do it! I'd lost count of how many times I'd said that in the phone call to him, and I'd buttered him up more than Fanny Craddock's cake tin. See, Mark wasn't a DJ. He knew his music but wasn't a DJ. Mark was the lighting jock and would only step in front of the decks if I had nipped to the toilet and wasn't back in time or to turn up the monitor speakers to deafen us if he liked a tune that was playing. So now, as you can probably imagine, he was thrown into the deep end, much to his annoyance, which he made evidently clear. He was most likely feeling the way I did when I arrived in the studios at Energy FM on that morning of my first day.

Mark, unbelievably still went ahead with this new plan which genuinely surprised me as I really thought that this was the straw that broke the camel's back. With a rough, and I mean rough, plan set in place, absolutely no hope of me returning for this gig, and Mark's temper one fowl word off needing therapy, I spent the remaining week in my spare time compiling a spreadsheet playlist for him to follow at this gig. It had what tracks to play and what CD it could be found on, and a rough order to play them in. I literally mapped out the whole gig's worth of music. It was a bloody long, laborious, and mind-numbing job, but it was the least I could do for him to try and put him in the shallows a little. On the day of the gig, I was working at the broadcast, and every free moment I had, I'd be checking my phone for any missed calls from the team back home setting up for the gig. I didn't get a single call off any of them, which could only mean that, luckily, there were no more issues arising. Either that, or they were all planning on how to bury me when I next saw them. I was absolutely devastated I couldn't make it back, and not a moment that went past that evening. I didn't think about how the team were getting on back there. I actually really missed them all.

I wanted to call them when my day was done with work, but I couldn't bring myself to it. I thought I'd just leave them to do it.

The following day I did call Mark to see how it all went, Mark did sound shattered, was still quite hostile towards me, and did still manage to find some more obscenities to call me that he had forgotten to say the previous day, but he then proceeded to say that they triumphed though and all pulled together well which I was very happy about and Mark pulled off his first and last solo gig. I was just thankful it wasn't the last gig he'd ever do with me. I'm pretty sure he had a good amount of free beer from me for the foreseeable. I did try to humour him and congratulate him for becoming a DJ overnight with a crash course over the phone, but that wasn't welcomed either and just resulted in a final round of more expletives being fired before cutting me off. Boy, did I have some sort of making-up to do. When I think back now, I find it very funny thinking back to our conversation; poor Mark was probably thinking, when is Ant and Dec going to appear to tell him it was just a wind-up as part of their Saturday night takeaway show? Thankfully thereon after, I never put him in a situation like that ever again; if there was a gig that I couldn't do for any reason, that was that.

As much as I loved my job in radio and working at Energy FM, the people I met, the people I worked with, and the Island itself, hand on heart, I don't think I ever really, truly settled there, and with me still being so busy with Mystikal Productions and club DJing back on the mainland it all became a little too much to juggle and it was inevitable that one day I'd return home there. Which I did after my initial six-month contract came to an end and up for renewal. It was a long, hard, and tough decision to make, but I decided that I wasn't going to renew and instead would return home, continue with gigs there and go back to the Shropshire Fire and Rescue service.

They do say home is where the heart is, and it was the first time in my life that such a saying rang true to me. I returned back home shortly afterward and picked up what I'd put on hold. I walked back into my role as a firefighter in the fire service, continued to DJ, which didn't include a plane flight, and pestered my old boss for my courier job back, which he agreed to after asking me if I was planning to stay this time, obviously because this wasn't a radio job, I couldn't guarantee anything I told him, but I'll see what I can do for the time being. I was always very honest, perhaps a little too honest at times. He did, though, have me back for a good solid 11 months before I left again for new pastures, which was a new record for me and no surprise to him.

Chapter 21
Popcorn with the Caribbean Queen

I returned home, back to Shrewsbury from the Isle of Man at the end of September 2011, and by December of that year, things were pretty all much back to normal and stable again like I'd never left. I was now working in two local clubs at weekends in between doing gigs around Shropshire with Mystikal Productions. You'll be pleased to know that Mark and I were back on good terms, and his torrent of rage towards me had subsided with a mass amount of good anger management therapy. The one club I was a resident DJ in was called C:21 back then, it's since changed its name to Havana Republic, I'd worked in this club now for several years with fellow DJs Rob Mulliner, Colin Matty, and Martin Luther (not that Martin Luther) on rotation.

The second club I got work in was The Buttermarket nightclub in Shrewsbury, which was a five-minute walk from where I now lived. The Buttermarket is a huge Grade II listed building that was built in 1835 and was a former butter warehouse. Years later, that became a nightclub which then shut down again after several years of trading. In 2012 the Buttermarket was bought by the same people that owned C:21 (Havana Republic), and it was given an extensive overhaul which, when opened, instantly put it on the map as a super club. It's a very impressive nightclub that draws hundreds of clubbers each and every week. With it being so big and being a super club, it was no surprise that they would have many famous acts and DJs perform here.

Mart, who used to DJ at the Havana Republic, made a move up to the Buttermarket to become the main Saturday night resident DJ. Rob, Colin, and I remained working at Havana but would also head up to The Buttermarket when they opened more rooms up or to cover on specific nights. Rob also hosted some '90s nights there, too, which were huge. I was lucky enough to play the main room several times, which was mind-blowing for me as this was by far the biggest club venue I'd ever played, not to mention the loudest with a bloody great Funktion One sound system which was about 15m high on each side of the stage. A guilty pleasure of mine from back in the day was the boy band 5ive. I take no shame in saying that I loved their music and still do, and much of their music was always in my sets from way back when. I was made up when asked to be the support DJ for one member of 5ive, Abz Love, when he came to perform. It was brilliant, well I thought so anyway; there were times during his performance that I was so tempted to grab a spare microphone and join him on stage to 'slam dunk the funk' and pretend I was a member of 5ive, luckily though, I resisted. Nice to see my willpower had returned, and just at the right time, thankfully.

Another random evening I had there was when Billy Ocean was touring and had been booked to play at the Buttermarket, which was also a night I was working there, and I managed to end up discussing with him which popcorn flavour was the best, because if you were, one day, to be found sharing a box of popcorn with the '80s music legend that is Billy Ocean in a dressing room backstage, wouldn't you want to iron out that matter? No, I'm hoping not, and neither did I really, but it broke the ice.

I'd finished a warm-up DJ set downstairs in a different room called the Cellars, it was an early door set, so when I had finished that, I grabbed a beer and then went up to the main room where Mr Ocean was doing his show. I'd popped backstage and up to the DJ box where my mate Sam Young was doing the lighting controls for the evening. After chewing the fat, I then made a quick visit to the toilet, where I passed Mr Oceans' dressing room, the door was open, and he was in there having a snack during half time. I casually walked past his dressing room, stopped, had a very quick think, then slowly walked back. I couldn't just ignore this, as this man is a musical legend. So, I took my chances to say hello as I'll never get this opportunity again, will I?

A quick chat about his evening and his hugely successful career would have broken the ice fine, then perhaps followed by an autograph and a photo perhaps? That would have been sufficient for most and an easy place to start a conversation and end it without pestering the man, but instead, the only conversation and the only time I'd ever meet this man, we spent a valuable, brief amount of time talking popcorn flavours. What a prize plum I am. Nevertheless, it was the best popcorn conversation I ever had, and I thoroughly enjoyed the well-spent use of time with him. He's a very pleasant man and, from what I gathered, enjoyed the chat, too, he was definitely pleased to have met me that night, and I did get a photo, too, which was nice. I was never the best at interviews, and they were most definitely my weak point. The most frustrating thing is, though, I can't remember what flavour of popcorn he preferred.

Now, I mentioned my mate Sam back there. Another top man is Sam, and that's where our friendship first started. I first met Sam whilst working at the Buttermarket; he swapped between DJing there himself and doing the lighting in the main room. Over my time working there I got to know him more, and it came to light that he was just starting out as a mobile DJ too, which I was only too happy to help him with. As he was just starting out, he had limited gear, and it reminded me of the time when Mark and I started. I was instantly reminded of how tough it was to get enough equipment together and to get gigs, and without the help of Dave Cornish way back then, I'd of never have gotten off the ground with it, so really, it was my opportunity and duty I felt to give something back and help Sam. The good and most important thing was Sam had already got a best friend of his to help him with his gigs, just like I had with Mark. Sam's best friend Matt was onboard and was keen to help Sam which was a great start. It was almost a mirror image of myself and Mark. Lets just hope they had a little more success and less drama with their beginnings! Mark and I both stepped in and helped Sam out with loaning equipment when he got booked for gigs and whilst he built up his own collection of equipment. Sam did very well from the start and was getting plenty of bookings which was great to see.

This worked really well for all of us as time went on, Sam would get booked for his own gigs, and Mark and I would give him any equipment he wanted for free, and in return, Sam and Matt were only too happy to assist us on the big gigs we did because any extra help on those was always appreciated and it also gave Sam some extra experience too. This also gave Mark a little more free time on the wedding and birthday gigs we did; if Mark wasn't able to make a gig, Sam would join me, and we would double up together and do it instead. Sam did tell me a story, though, which I found hilarious and couldn't help but think was it our curse put upon him on one of his gigs. Sam and Matt had borrowed a pair of giant flame machines from us for a wedding gig he had on. These flame machines were just a box with a fan, some red and blue LEDs, and a 2m piece of silk which, when switched on, would give quite an effective display of a flame. Back then, these were quite a centrepiece, and you wanted to save them for a jaw-dropping moment during the night, which Sam and Matt did. Well... they got their jaw-dropping moment, alright. Sam and Matt were thinking creatively, exactly like Mark and I would have done; they saved switching the flames on until mid-way through the first dance at the wedding they were doing. Great idea.

These flame machines, you'd switch them on at the box, and then a remote control would kick them into life. Sam started playing the first dance song of choice whilst Matt ducked down and hid out of sight behind the deck stand; then, at the penultimate moment, Sam gave Matt the thumbs up to trigger the flames with the remotes. In what should have been a magical romantic moment turned quickly into a massive anti-climax. Those flames didn't spring up and look jaw-dropping. Instead, they tripped the fuse box of the venue, and the dance floor fell silent and dark! As Sam was telling me this, I couldn't help but laugh and, at the same time, felt the utter panic he and Matt would have done. I can just imagine Sam standing there not knowing what to do whilst Matt, on his knees, hiding behind the DJ booth, not really wanting to get back up. All I could see was Mark and me in the exact same situation, just standing there praying that someone would flick the switch as quickly as possible whilst I was going for a world record in how many times you can utter the word 'bollocks' in 30 seconds.

Mark checked those flame lamps over for any issues, but he found none, so the issue lay somewhere else that evening. However, those flame lamps never came out on the road again with us and certainly never went out with Sam and Matt to a gig, either. They were classed as boxes of doom. Flame lamps aside, this new business venture between us was working perfectly, we continued to get booked for all the regular gigs we had annually and were picking up new ones, too, we had room to expand too with bigger rigs as we had Sam and Matt giving us help and Sam had started to buy his own gear too which we added to our rig, so it was really quite something. It also got to the point where Mark and I could take on two separate gigs on the same night, and we could go and do one of them while Sam and Matt went and did another. Business was booming!

A few years later, Sam and I left The Buttermarket; Mart was holding the residency there, Sam got really busy with his gigs and couldn't commit to doing the lighting anymore, and I was now either working our own gigs or was DJing in Havana. Although no sooner had I stepped out of one club, It wasn't long before I'd find myself back over in Mid Wales in another club. In December 2014, I got a call from Dave asking me a question…would I like to be added to the DJ roster to DJ in the club he did in Mid Wales. Was I hearing this correctly? Dave asked me if I wanted to DJ in the same club as him.

The reason I was surprised was a bit of a running joke we had for years before this call, probably as far back as 2004; it could have been more, perhaps, right back to when I first started to DJ and long before I was working as a DJ in a club. For at least 10 years, I'd been pestering Dave for a gig at this club, Crystals Nightclub, it was called; he was a very honest man and sometimes would just give me a blunt no or maybe one day followed with a big grin. I didn't quite understand why he wouldn't say yes.

I remember once, in my quest to get Dave to give me a shot, he told me to record a demo for him, so with excitement, I did just that. I recorded a whole gig live and direct on to Mini-Disc; remember those? I recorded about five hours of me DJing and thought that I should do it. It didn't. In fact, Dave didn't give me any feedback whatsoever on them either, which didn't surprise me. When I think about it, I'm adamant he didn't even listen to them as I saw the mini-discs I'd given him on the dashboard of his Range Rover many months after where he put them when I handed them over to him, and he certainly didn't have a mini-disc player in that.

It didn't make much sense to me back then why he wouldn't give me a shot, but in later years, it did make sense; he was a professional and, just like Austin making me record demo radio shows until the time came he felt I was ready, Dave was doing exactly the same in the club world, he was letting me get on with getting experience under my belt until one day I was ready to step up to the plate. By the time his call came in, I'd done umpteen gigs of all sizes and shapes on the road and had been DJing in several clubs in Shrewsbury, so in Dave's eyes, I guess he thought I was ready and had gained plenty of experience by now.

December 2014, I gladly accepted the invite onto the roster of DJs for Crystals nightclub, I was really looking forward to starting a new chapter there; Crystals was a club that I always used to go to years ago for a night out before I moved to Shrewsbury, so I knew what to expect. Crystals nightclub was inside a grand building called the Regent Centre which was at the top of Broad Street in Newtown, Powys. The club was on one side of the building, and there was a cinema on the other side. Off the street, you'd walk up some steep steps to the doors of the club and enter a nice large reception room where you'd pay your entry fee, and get branded with the classic ink stamp before walking through a dark corridor over the classic sticky carpet and into the very large main room, had an array of lighting all around the dance floor and a really good sized DJ booth. If you like your history, much like the Buttermarket in Shrewsbury, The Regent Centre was originally built in

1830 and was used as a flannel exchange; what a flannel exchange exactly is. I don't really know. Although there's a pub underneath the Regent Centre called The Exchange, which is a nice little nod to its history, I'm glad they changed the club's name. If someone asked you what you were doing this weekend and you said that you were off to the flannel exchange, they would probably envisage you heading out to buy some new bits for your bathroom or heading to some form of Roman-themed orgy.

Anyhow, I knew what to expect at Crystals when I arrived there that night in regards to the kind of people that went and the music policy; what I didn't expect was the selection test Dave was to put me through before leaving me to DJ. I found this highly amusing; Dave was super professional, and if he was vouching for you, you had to be up to his standards. New Year's Eve 2014, and I had arranged to go to the club, but I wasn't to DJ this particular night; I was to be with Dave in the DJ box for the duration to watch, learn and soak up the atmosphere and observe with a keen eye how Dave did things in his town, which was fine, I didn't mind, it was nice to watch him DJ again after several years and catch up with him properly as I didn't see all that much of him.

After New Year's Eve was done and we were into 2015, The next gig Dave asked me to do, I turned up, and he gave me the debrief to phase two of the selection tests. For this gig, Dave was to DJ half of the night, and then I was to DJ the second half of the evening whilst he then took a step back and observed me. I did find this difficult because I had to use his music collection, which was a library of every song in the world. Trying to navigate another DJs music library is like flying a submarine. It's tough. With your own music library, you know where everything is and in some form of order. Dave did understand this and appreciated the advanced level of difficulty. Again this gig was completed successfully, and another test was ticked off.

So, we landed at phase three of Dave's selection test. This next gig he booked me for, I was to play the entire evening, the moment I was waiting for and thinking to myself that I must have passed the test by now. I met Dave in the DJ booth, and he gave me the debrief; he then said that he was going to leave me for the evening. Once Dave had left, I began to relax and get into the swing of the evening; as much as I loved Dave, having someone watching over you who's hired, you is the pressure you could do without.

The night was going great, the music was thumping, and I had and maintained a full dance floor, but what's this? I was looking out over the dance floor and just happened to catch a glimpse of a figure dive behind a pillar that I could have sworn was Dave. No, it couldn't have been; I said goodbye to him earlier, and he's left me to do the night and gone home for a nice cup of warm water or something like that.

But hang about; I'm sure I've just seen him up on the balcony now, which overlooked the DJ booth!? At this point, I thought I was losing my mind, and the selection test Dave had put me through had long-lasting mental effects on me. I carried on, questioning myself and my sanity then it wasn't long until again, this time, my attention was diverted to the back door behind the bar, when…like a game of hide and seek, I caught a full view of Dave craftily watching me, it was at this point he knew he was rumbled, and he stood there with the biggest grin on his face I'd ever seen, whilst he lip-read some explicit language from me, he hadn't left the club and gone home, his phase three of the test was to secretly blend in with the club and literally go from pillar to post monitoring my DJ set. The absolute git! But again, nothing surprised me coming from Dave. From then on, whenever I did a gig there, Mark, who then joined me on each club gig, used to keep an eye out for the invisible Dave, you just never knew which part of the furniture he'd spring up from and make an appearance. The twit.

From then on, though, I had firmly secured myself as a resident DJ at Crystals nightclub on the roster of DJs. Finally, after years and years of wanting to play at this club, I was and felt a great sense of achievement. I also got my mini-discs back too, and if I could find them again, somewhere, they still have my original demo on them.

Chapter 22
A Stark Reality

When we set out mobile DJing, we were always happy and willing to receive any booking for any kind of event, but there were always a few events that we attended as punters that we would always say to each other that we really wanted to do one day. One of those was the YFC Chairman's Ball, which was undoubtedly the biggest gig of each year; it was a monumental-sized gig where hundreds and hundreds of members from YFC clubs from miles around would all congregate for the biggest party of the year to celebrate the chairman of the YFC. The only thing missing was people wearing animal masks and a giant wicker man on fire in the field.

A few years into mobile DJing and after numerous ordinary YFC gigs under our belts, I'm happy to report we got one of these gigs, which was held locally to us; I think if my memory serves me correctly, it was the summer of 2006. It was held just up the road from where I lived at the time in Clun and was in a colossal marquee that spanned off in all different directions. I also remember that us being us, we had to fill every corner with some form of lighting to bring it to life, so we split our rig into four parts and scattered it all around the marquee, which was hard work, but it looked pretty amazing. Standard just wasn't a word in our dictionary when it came to setting up a rig, no matter how much extra work it caused Mark. We would visualise what we wanted to do, like lighting architects, and then Mark would bugger off and set about constructing extra custom-made bits in his workshop. I'm certain on this particular gig we were hanging lighting off some thin diameter roof struts, and our lighting clamps were too big for them, so Mark overcame that issue quite easily by cutting up a car tire, and we padded them out with the rubber from it. So whilst the party people were going for it on the dance floor that evening, they were totally unaware that above them, there were the scattered parts of an Avon ZX7.

At the time, we were still using some UV lights too, which were six-foot kitchen tube lights recovered from a skip by Mark with the standard lighting tube removed and UV tubes replaced. These, I remember, were mounted vertically on the lighting stands. Again, these were modified by Mark by wiring them up with electrical cable and putting a plug on the end; it was only natural the fixing mechanism of these were car exhaust clamps, more than likely borrowed from my dad's garage, which were probably parts he needed for a repair later that week.

Anyway, that was one big gig ticked off the list, and secondly, the other ultimate gig we wanted to play was a gig called The Burwarton Show after-party. This was always another huge gig, quite possibly the next biggest gig down from the chairman's Ball. One year we'd ventured over to one of these gigs for some reconnaissance to see what it was all about. It didn't disappoint. It was also held again in a huge marquee in the evening after an annual agricultural show. The place would be filled to bursting point with YFC members ready to blow off some steam; you're talking in excess of 2000 plus people? And let me tell you, after a hot sunny day at an agriculture show, drinking gallons of cider all day, these young farmers were ready to party hard and wild, and they certainly did just that. Maniacs.

This was a gig we had to have a go at doing someday, we thought, but with a regular DJ already booked each year to play, it was extremely hard to get a shot at it, despite advertising in the YFC annual handbook and sending letters out to each YFC club in Shropshire and already having played many of their gigs, we just couldn't break down the wall and get our chance, that was until the summer of 2013, this was it, the wall started to crumble it seemed and our time to shine presented itself, and we were called up to the stand. This was very important to us, and it was also very important that we pulled out all the stops for this gig, as we wanted to continue having this firmly penciled into our diary year after year. So we checked all of our gear, got Sam's gear, got Dave's gear, and made sure that we had an extra car tire at hand, just in case.

So, how did we get this gig like a bolt out of the blue? Well, I remember why, it wasn't because we advertised and it wasn't because I sent out letters, all in all, it came down to the basics and how fussy we were in having to have the best equipment, funnily enough. It was down to us constantly reinvesting the money we made from gigs into new equipment and never taking a cut of it for ourselves. We always had to save to afford the best in the market, and although we thought we were daft and most other people thought the same, it eventually paid off, and this was the day it did.

Let me explain; going back to the gigs with Radio 1 DJs we did, if you're unfamiliar with how the admin side works, once a celebrity DJ is booked and, like any other celebrity booked to do something, they have what they call a rider, which is just a list of luxuries/requirements/extras they would like for when they attend the gig. For example, when I met Billy Ocean and sat eating popcorn with him, he may very well of asked for popcorn on his rider. When we had Scott Mills join us for a gig, he requested a fresh towel, bottled water, and snacks, which we then had to provide for him. What a celebrity requests on their rider is completely up to them. Sometimes it's relatively cheap, and other times it can add to the expense. For example, they can request to be put up in a hotel for the evening, so it varies widely. As well as all these little extras for the celeb, the agency will request a list of equipment that is required. If you don't have the DJ equipment required, the chances are they won't get booked. Usually, and at no surprise, it's the most expensive, most up-to-date DJ decks and mixer that they specify, Pioneer CDJ 2000 and a Pioneer DJM800 (at the time), which is high-end gear and normally only found in clubs and for a mobile outfit, at the cost of these, not getting much change from £2000 per unit, not many would have this spec of equipment, but there was one mobile outfit that did, us.

I honestly can't remember the DJ the YFC used at the time for the Burwarton After Show Party, but as a BBC Radio 1 guest DJ was becoming a popular thing at large events like these, the YFC had come up trumps again and had managed to book Radio 1's Chris Stark who was Scott Mills on-air right-hand man who is fantastic. The YFC had asked the previous DJ to play, but unfortunately, he didn't have the equipment specified by the agency and turned down the gig on the basis of that, and I'm pretty sure he kindly told the YFC to get in contact with us as we had already got experience with working with BBC Radio 1 DJs. The YFC then called us and explained what was happening and whether we have the equipment specified. Luckily for us, we did, and with that easy answer, the contract was signed, and we were ready to put our stamp, along with Chris Stark, on The Burwarton Show After Party. Get in.

Right then, there was to be no holding back on this gig. It was all hands to deck; every single last piece of equipment and cable came out of the lock-up for this, and we doubled up speaker power too. It was that grand a setup, and we drew in the extra help again, Sam and Martin from the Buttermarket. In true fashion, Mark created the extra hard work for himself with his 3D 360 plans of hanging lighting from anywhere it was possible to hang lighting from strewn all the way down the roof lining of this giant marquee. There was never any concern about the weight of all these lighting fixtures; as long as they went up and stayed up for a good six hours, we were winning. At this time in our career, Mark had built himself a very technical computer-based lighting programme controller, which was impressive. It was basically a PC in a flight case with a touch screen. He could now control all the lights with this and also mock up a diagram on the computer of a lighting rig and see how it would look before you set it up, which was really handy. The clever sausage.

The setup took pretty much all day to get into place; by the time we had setup, we had just about enough time to get home, showered, fed, and watered before heading back to play.

What I did find very helpful was pre-planning music, and DJ sets with Chris Stark before the event. We exchanged several text messages in the week leading up to the event, discussing my warm-up set, what he was planning on playing, what to avoid, etc. This, as I say, was very useful and helpful. As a professional DJ warming up before the main DJ at an event, you should never go in all guns blazing and play all the big hitters, as you'll find the main DJ/guest DJ will be playing those most of the time. So if you can, always speak to the DJ that follows you to get an idea of what they intend to play and how you can craft your warm-up set to blend into theirs without stepping on their toes. This is a golden rule as a warm-up DJ, not to be forgotten. If you can, always try to contact the DJ following you, just to be on the safe side and to make sure you both know the script. Doing that isn't always possible, so you'll just have to use your common sense and play safe.

The night came and went extremely quickly; the marquee was jam-packed, the vibe was awesome, and again, it was another sell-out event. Sam and I crafted a back-to-back warm-up set before Chris played, getting everyone hyped up, and then Chris came on a rocked the place with his set. He really was a fantastic DJ, a great host, and an absolute pleasure to work with. Mark pulled out all the stops with his light jocking and gave one hell of a light show, the best I'd ever seen, to be honest! And then, once Chris had finished his set, Sam and I continued to DJ to keep the place bouncing until the end. The whole gig was electric from start to finish. Top drawer chaps. I was very happy, in general how the night played out; everything went as it should have. It was about this time in our mobile DJ career that all boners seemed to have ceased, and we actually went gig to gig from start to end with no mishaps or nasty surprises lurking around every corner, ready to jump out at us. I think we were, by now, actually professional. I was happy knowing that we all came together that night to give it our all, and we did just that; no sooner had that gig finished than there was one thing on our minds. Have we secured this gig now?

Once the gig was all over, we all met up and had a beer together the following day, talking it all over, like a debrief if you like, and left wandering if we had secured our place at next year's Burwarton Show. Well, I'm pleased to say that due to its success, we were booked for the following year (2014), and to our delight, Chris Stark would be joining us again. Happy days. The Burwarton Show 2014 was equally as successful as the previous one and just as tiring! But all very much well worth it. In 2015, We were booked to play again, no Chris Stark this time, but instead, we were to be joined by a different BBC Radio 1 DJ, the wonderful Alice Levine. Sadly though, this was to be the last time we did this gig. I can't quite remember why we didn't do it the following year; all I can remember, though, is that they didn't have a Radio 1 DJ at that event, so I'd like to think they handed the reigns back over to the DJ that used to do them before we had our spell there. We completed three gigs at Burwarton, all of which were superb, and we were all very grateful to be given the opportunity to play them. The dances at the Burwarton are still held each and every year to date.

By the closing of 2015, we had some fantastic big gigs under our belts, and we had finally ticked off all the gigs we really wanted to play, which was an outstanding achievement. We really felt that we'd done what we always wanted to do. Even though I still wasn't a firm fix on BBC Radio 1 as a regular DJ, I had, by now, realised that this was just another dream I had that was just that little too difficult to get. Although I had been tremendously lucky working with Greg James, Scott Mills, Chris Stark, JK and Joel, Aled Haydn Jones, and Alice Levine, who were all BBC Radio 1 DJs, and at the end of the last gig we did with Chris Stark, I did a recording with him which was played out on the Scott Mills show. So I may have never got to BBC Radio 1, but I was certainly lucky enough to meet my idols that lived that dream of theirs, and with that, that's close enough in my book to be extremely content and grateful for. As much as we loved to play these big expanded gigs and had done for several years, something quite odd was beginning to creep in following them, fatigue. We were really beginning to feel the pinch of them.

Chapter 23
The Closing of The Curtain

Here, we find ourselves in 2016—17 years as a mobile entertainment outfit and 16 years as Mystikal Productions.

As we landed into 2016, we were out on the road still providing mobile entertainment on large scales and holding down two DJ residencies in nightclubs, but things were slowly and naturally changing direction. Club gigs in Shrewsbury were busy and equally as busy in the other club in Mid Wales; however, by the summer of 2016, the mobile gigs seemed to be slowing down some. We did agree between ourselves. I think in 2015 when we were playing lots of the large events, we wouldn't be doing wedding or birthday events no more, we were just mainly focusing more on YFC events and club work, but even the YFC events started to slow down. It was a combination of fewer gigs being organised and 'new blood' coming through, where new DJs were coming through the system to provide the entertainment, just like it did when we arrived on the circuit, which was great because personally, I thought it was a good thing that some younger DJs were starting out their journey as we did and just like the Take That lyrics in Never Forget. They sang, "Someday, this will be someone else's dream," and it was for someone, which was really nice to see.

It was evident that we did lose some gigs to a new outfit, but we were never ever bitter about it. We respected that and wished them all the success with it. At an early stage, I learned never to be upset about other fellow DJs; they chose to go on the same journey we did, and if they get a gig, then all the best to them. Everyone deserves to have a shot at the game. We had another annual gig in our books for several years, which was another large YFC gig, it was The Newport After Show Party, which was pretty much identical to the previously mentioned Burwarton Show.

This was a fantastic gig that we looked forward to every July in a huge warehouse on a remote farm, and just like the Burwarton Show, this gig followed after an all-day agricultural show in Newport, Shropshire, so you were always guaranteed a flood of thirsty farmers through the doors ready for a good party. It was a brilliant venue, stacked full of potato boxes which, naturally, we used to our advantage to illuminate with LED uplighting and prop further lighting on expanding our rig. Mark could make the most of anything!

We had done this gig for. I think, four years? And we were set for the same gig in 2016. We always said to each other, whilst setting up for a gig, I wonder when our last gig will be?

At the time, and unknowingly to us, this was to be it; the 2016 Newport Aftershow Party was to be our final mobile gig out as Mystikal Productions. I think we were both at a stage in life where we had both got a lot of commitments with work and normal, boring grown-up things to start dealing with. We both started at a very young age which was great and the right time to do it, as nothing else mattered or was more important than doing a gig, we literally lived for the weekend, and we really did smash out the whole mobile thing the best we possibly could. Mark was busy with his day job, which also required him to work every other weekend. I was finally, after long last, believe it or not, holding down a full-time job that I actually enjoyed and was successfully sticking with. I was now also qualified to drive the fire truck, which meant I had to be on call more often, which restricted my weekends some.

As I mentioned before, life on the road was getting tougher and more demanding, we could have cut down on our rigs, but that was never an option for us, go big or go home was how we looked at it. And with not wanting to cut down on our rig size and, therefore, a large-scale gig becoming a 24-hour operation, they were certainly more tiring, and our energy levels were depleting, not that we ever and never will accept that we were getting older, but we could really feel the years of doing this job catching up with us, not the DJing, just the long, hard manual labour and long nights/mornings these gigs turned into. I remember actually being shocked after this particular gig; getting home and looking at the time, I made a point of staying up an extra 10 minutes after getting home to round off a 24-hour day of work. I or we started to realise that we couldn't keep this up at the weekend and then return to work on a Monday morning, no matter how much fun it was. This was a little sad but a natural occurrence that we made peace with. All the other lads had gone their own ways at weekends too by this point so it was left to myself, Mark, and Sam, when in reality for the amount of work that was involved, a crew of 6 to 10 would have been what was needed.

We also found that we had started to decline gigs and weren't as enthusiastic to accept them knowing how much work was to follow and us being us, it was all or nothing, we would much rather decline a gig than do it half hearted, and, used to working in clubs now, it was far less stress and much easier to walk into a Club 30mins before your set, play and then walk out again 10mins after you'd finished. Mark always said to me, "This is an easier way to do it mate," and I had to agree; it was, and the luxury of DJing the clubs was becoming our much preferred gig.

We had always imagined that we would announce our retirement from the mobile circuit, putting on one big party to finish it all and draw a line under it, hire the big speakers, extra lighting, some pyrotechnics, etc. But that wasn't to be, and in fact, thinking about it, I don't think that would have worked. It would have obviously been too staged, and all the way through the gig we'd be thinking, this is it! The finale! And knowing Mark and I, we would really disappoint ourselves! But instead, what did happen was just a normal big gig to us, no pyrotechnics, no announcements and no thoughts in the back of our minds that this would be the last mobile gig we do.
Instead, what we do have to mark it is a perfect photo that I took of Marks silhouette standing by his beloved lighting controller, It really is a moment of 'unintentional perfection', as I call it. And personally, I think it draws a line under all those years perfectly. You could have taken 1000 photos trying to get that perfect last photo, but you'd of never of gotten one like this, and all I did was grab a quick photo for no apparent reason just before I got back onto the stage.

I can't and never will remember the first track we ever played at our very first gig together as Mystikal Productions, and I dread to think, but thankfully I can remember the final tracks we played on our final mobile gig: 'Little Lion Man' by Mumford & Sons and 'You've Got The Love' by Florence and The Machine; 'Changing' by Sigma ft. Paloma Faith was the final track that officially closed the curtain for us, and to this day, that track holds special sentimental memories for myself, Mark, and Sam. Ever since its release in 2014, that track was always used to close our DJ sets, as it just harnesses a powerful high to end on.

With that gig at Newport completed at 2:00 a.m., we played our final track, and we signed off for the last time as Mystikal Productions, and with that, Mystikal Productions, there and then, was put to bed in July of 2016. So, what happened next, then? What did the future hold now for us all? And what were we going to do going forward with us retired from the mobile circuit? After that gig, Mark and I didn't disappear into the night in a puff of smoke, we may have called time on the road, but for the following few years, you could still come and see us DJing in a nightclub in Shrewsbury or Newtown, we were still very busy most weekends.

The nightclub in Shrewsbury I played, C:21, that closed short term for a huge refit and rebrand, which emerged as Havana Republic, a Cuban-inspired bar. When the refit was completed, they had taken a slightly different direction and closed the other room, Spirit, as a general nightclub and second room, instead, it was used mainly for private functions and Christmas parties and only opened if the Havana side was at capacity. Naturally, with this change in direction, two DJs at the weekend were no longer required unless they had a private party, etc. Therefore, my time there as a resident DJ had come to an end as Colin was the main DJ there, continuing to play weekends in Havana.

Crystals nightclub in Newtown? At the time, the current management, Luke, had decided to call last orders as reigning management and move on to new pastures. Sadly the club was to be closed for the foreseeable with no certain future ahead of it. Myself and Mark played the very last night there on Saturday, 22nd December 2017. Its since been reopened and rebranded as The Steam Mill and today continue to provide Mid Wales with a thriving nightclub. It is under management by the same management that also has another nightclub called Molto in the next town down from Newtown in Welshpool. I've not played there since Crystals shut.

After I lost these two residencies and had called time on the road, It was looking pretty quiet on the DJ front. It was nice to have every weekend now free to concentrate on other things, but after some time away from it, I had an itch that needed to be scratched. I didn't quite know what to do with myself in regards to DJing as this was the first time in 20 years I didn't have any gigs to do in my diary, which was really strange. Sam had gotten himself onto a DJ agency called Diamond UK Promotions, run by the hugely talented DJ Tony Tee. Tony would book Sam for gigs all over, including Molto nightclub in Welshpool, and with the Molto management now running The Steam Mill, Sam also played there through Tony. Well, it was always going to happen; after a few talks, I got myself onto the agency, too, and was sent out and about DJing again via Tony. This was a fantastic way to keep yourself busy with gigs. I did DJ in Molto several times in Welshpool, but didn't actually ever return to The Steam Mill. I'm pleased to say that Mark would join me again when I did these gigs, which was really nice and a great opportunity to catch up with him again. With the downtime I had between DJing and getting on the agency, I figured that I found lots of things to do at weekends and couldn't really commit to as many gigs anymore as I'd have liked to, so after a spell with Diamond UK Promotions I stepped back to concentrate on other commitments.

I personally think that if you're a DJ and have a connection to it like Mark, Sam, and I do, together or as a solo DJ, you'll never stop doing what you do. You may hang up the headphones from time to time or just take things a little slower and space out your gigs a little, but it will always be in your blood, and sooner or later, you'll return to it one way or another. To this very day, Mark and I are still the best of friends, and we meet up together when we have free time for a beer; and Mark can still usually be found at any gig I play. He's swapped roles now, though; instead of propping up against his lighting controller, it's usually the bar now. Marks kept busy with his day job and currently renovating a property he bought, which is due for completion in 2048. He has a lovely partner, Amanda, and they are expecting their first child in August 2023. He is still very much into his music and often sends me links at all hours to new tunes he's found and recommends I play in my next set. If you're curious to put a face to his name, take a closer look at the front cover of this book. Yes, that fine figure staring back at me is the man himself. Mark is still driving a Land Rover, and I've not put him in a bad mood for a very long time.

Sam, he's extremely busy as an electrician, he's now engaged to the lovely Abi, and they have just had a baby boy in April 2023. Sam and I still see each other regularly and have launched a new project together called Dance Anthems Takeover, which we started in January 2022. We were once again partnered up and DJing together again, which was brilliant. Although we have swapped the ungodly hours of the night and now DJ in the afternoon, that's what Dance Anthems Takeover is all about, afternoon clubbing. It's proving very successful. It's different from most gigs as, for one, it's in the afternoon, and secondly, we have our good friends Khyle and Liam on board with us, who are super talented photographers and videographers and have a business called Over The Moon Pictures. This is an exciting new venture for us, and it's so much fun to be working with all these guys together at these gigs. I'm just curious to see how long the afternoon gigs last before we start working back into the night time scene. I wish though, all those years back, we had Khyle and Liam onboard to document all the previous gigs we had done. The main thing is that they are firmly by our sides now going forward. I've not yet managed to annoy these lads.

As for me, somehow, after nearing 20 jobs on my CV, I finally managed to settle into full-time employment and get a good career in a job that I enjoy; no one would have believed that in the last years of the 19th century that human affairs were being watched from the timeless worlds of space. Oh, hang on, I'm back to The War of the Worlds again there! Sorry... No one would have believed that I'm still in the same job, going on 10 years now. I struggle to believe that fact myself.

The penny finally dropped, and I realised that a job, whether it be in radio or another career path, is quite an important thing in life. I met my wife, Emma, and two stepdaughters, Merci and Esme, and bought a house back in the country along with a mental dog called Peanut. I retired from the Shropshire Fire and Rescue Service in January 2017 after serving 15 years as an on-call retained firefighter.

I've been DJing for a total of 25 years, and I'm pleased to say that I'm still very much DJing. The headphones haven't been hung up yet.

So... my conclusion?

Did I complete my dreams of completing Sonic The Hedgehog 3, Work as a radio presenter, and becoming a firefighter? Yes, I did.

Did I ever make it to the top and become a top DJ like I dreamt? No, I didn't.

But...

Was I - or were we - successful in what I/we did? Yes, I think so.

We worked hard and tirelessly as a team of best friends, and as individuals. Hard work does pay off. We were professional (eventually) passionate and obsessive over quality in what we provided to the people and clients. We achieved far more than we ever imagined we would along the way; we had ups and downs, good gigs and not-so-good gigs, won gigs and lost gigs, made a profit, made a loss and broke even, we struggled and stressed, laughed and cried, met and worked with some fantastic people, met and worked with some idols and lost an unhealthy amount of sleep and ended up having to take supplements and use anti-aging moisturiser far too soon as a result, but I personally lived my dream and have zero regrets about any of the journey. Whether or not Mark did remains a mystery. Feel free to ask him. In fact, I may ask him to write a book from his version of events, that I would love to see.

We didn't get rich from our time entertaining but knew we never would. We were driven by the passion and the love of music, the industry, loyal friendship, and entertainment.

But let me tell you this: above all, what we did do, and most importantly, we did exactly what our mentor Dave Cornish had always told us to do… **"Have fun and party."**

And you know what? We loved every single bloody moment of it.

Cheers!

Dedicated to the loving memory of Dave Cornish
1960-2017

"Without you, there's no colour. Without you, there's no joy. No one to share fond memories of us girl and boy.

No more Ibiza sunsets, no more booming calls. No more shorts in winter, a strong arm when I fall.

No more chats and dog walks, remembering mum and dad. No more Christmas lighting and hugs when I was sad.

The person in my corner who loved me to the end. I love you to the end of time, my brother, rock, and friend."

Jen Cornish
(Dave's Sister)
xxxx

Photo credit – Crystals Nightclub

Dave Cornish

Dave was a truly wonderful man; sadly, he passed away unexpectedly in August 2017. It was a tremendous shock and loss to me and everyone who knew him. His passing was felt far and wide, leaving a huge void across mid-Wales and the club scene. Jenny, I've thoroughly enjoyed sharing my memories of your brother. Without Dave, I'd have never gotten off the ground with my mobile gigs or achieved as much as myself and Mark did, and in turn, in later years, I would never have had the content to write this book. When I decided to put pen to paper and try writing about my life as a DJ, Dave was my first thought and the driving force throughout to do this, and it felt only right to dedicate the book to him. I know if he was still with us and I handed this book to him to read, it would probably still be on the dashboard of his Range Rover, just like my mini-discs were. His ongoing and continued support to us was unforgettable. He really did look after us 24/7. I'm forever grateful that I got to meet and become friends with him. I speak for myself and many others he helped; he was a loyal, inspirational friend and role model and leaves a legacy. I have nothing but the best memories of him, and I always will. He is sorely missed.

Acknowledgements

Where do I even begin? Everyone mentioned in this book played a huge role in my life over the years when I was doing what I was doing.

Mark and Sam—thank you for always being by my side and going along with anything that I wanted to do and achieve. Your support and hard work were always appreciated. Thank you.

Lewis, Crangle, Rhys, and Rob—thank you for all the help and support you gave throughout years of various gigs of all shapes and sizes and being the best friends anyone could ever want.

Mum, Dad, and Jess—thank you for all the music (I pinched and ruined). The use and taxi services provided with the Volvo, and ultimately, buying a mobile disco.

Austin, Juan, and Andy—thank you all for being the dream makers and taking the chance to employ me to work on your radio stations, which I absolutely loved. I hold the best memories of each of these radio stations.

James, thank you for all you currently do with promoting Dance Anthems Takeover for us, and an extra special thank you for all your involvement with polishing up this book.

Khyle and Liam—thank you for all your exceptional work as Over The Moon Pictures at our Dance Anthems Takeover gigs and for capturing the perfect front cover for this book. You had no idea at the time, and neither did I, that the photo you captured there would become a book cover. Keep up the good work; you guys will go far.

Kevin Horak (DJ Mr. Wolf) and Carole Anne Carr—two fantastic authors who already have books released and available to buy—gave me their expert advice on everything book! Without the help and advice you gave me, this wouldn't be here now. Thank you both so much. Kev, I've not forgotten to spend some time with you DJing!

Emma, Merci, Esme—thank you for the support you have given me whilst I've been trying to write this ridiculous book. You always encouraged me to push forward with it, and when I first came to you and said I was going to write a book, you actually believed me and said I would, which was strange!

Thank you to all the management at all the clubs I have had the pleasure of working at over the years.

Thank you to all the members of the Shropshire Young Farmers Clubs for being loyal and booking us for many, many gigs over the years.

And lastly, thank you to absolutely everybody that I may have missed or met throughout this journey in the DJ world. You are all beautiful people.

Credits

Mark Richardson – Sam Young – Matt Wharton – Andy Lewis – Jon Crangle - Rob Hughes – Rhys Davies – Pete Reynolds – Pete Collins – Dan Harding – Al Williams – Graham Dudley – Jack Limond – The White Horse Inn, Clun – Shropshire Fire & Rescue Service – Steve Davies – Rob Ford - Johnny Francis – Anthony Francis – Jess Evans (Morris) – Ellie Lewis – Glenda Morris – John Morris – Dave Cornish – Jenny Cornish – Austin Powell – Juan Turner – Andy Walters – Alan Thompson – Colin Matty – Rob Mulliner – Mart Luther – Liam Christopher Davies – Khyle Manby Evans – James Brinkler – Carole Anne Carr – Kevin Horak - Tony Tee – Diamond Uk Management – Red Flame Electrical – Radio Maldwyn – Mike Baker – Adrian Lawley – Ashley Owen – Julian Saunders – Simon Doe – Mark Edwards – Martin Adams – Peter Birch – Energy FM – WCR FM – Heat FM – Pipeline Radio – Havana Republic – The Buttermarket – Crystals Nightclub – Luke Orehawa - The Steam Mill – Moltos Nightclub -The Wheatsheaf in Frankwell – The Shropshire Young Farmers Club – SPA Creative – Crossfader – Digital DJ Tips – Jonathan Lewis AKA Ellaskins The DJ Tutor – Club Ready DJ School – DJ Phil Harris – BBC Radio 1 – JK and Joel – Scott Mills – Greg James – Aled Haydn Jones – Chris Stark – Alice Levine – Abz Love – Billy Ocean – Sonic The Hedgehog and Dan Morris

Hints, Tips, and Other Bits

With my story complete, in this section, I wanted to share some advice and some things I learnt as a DJ. It's a bit of a whistle-stop tour, and that's how I want it to be.
My intention is to give you some real, honest advice and pointers on where to go next for further, more in-depth information after I have given you some basic advice and tips to get you started. For example, I'd love to be able to teach you how to beat mix, but that would be quite difficult without a practical demonstration, so instead, I'll point you in the direction of some fantastic places that can teach you.

To anyone reading this who's thinking about following the same path I/we did, it's simple: do it.

I have no regrets about any part of my journey. DJing is an amazing experience, and once you've had a break and played to a crowd of people for the first time, be it 10 at a house party or 1000 at a large event, once you witness people dancing and having a good time to what you're playing, there's no better feeling, and let me tell you, once you've had that experience, you'll be hooked.

If you're already a DJ and have experience in the following, you may just want to skip this part and give the book to a friend or a charity shop. I'm writing this primarily for anyone reading who is a complete beginner and thinking about starting their journey as a DJ.

In this part of the book, I'll be writing about my own personal experiences, what I was taught, and what advice and actions I took. I'm not saying you must follow what I did, and none of the following should be used as financial advice, but I'm hoping some of the advice will help you get started in some way, as it did me. In this day and age, it is a million times easier to get the information and help needed to get you where you want to be. You just need to know where to look, and I'll point you to some places that I found extremely useful and helpful.

What kind of DJ do you want to be?

Have a think about this one; this is something that you'll only know and need to figure out in good time, but don't rush and force yourself into something you know you won't be happy with. Take your time and figure out who you are and what you want to play. You may find you'll have to do all sorts of different types of events and experiment until you click with what suits you. When I say what kind of DJ you want to be, I don't mean what you want to DJ on, such as vinyl turntables, CDJs, or controllers. I mean, what kind of events and music do you want to play.

When I started, I was into club/trance/dance/house music, and a whole host of other genres, and I still am. I did think to begin with that I'd be a Dance DJ as I grew up listening to Judge Jules and Dave Pearce, among other dance DJs on BBC Radio 1. That's primarily what I do now after my years on the road as a mobile DJ. I've come back after 25 years of DJing, only now to solely focus on DJing Dance music and the dance music that I love and have a passion for—both past and present.

In the beginning, I chose, or should I say, fell into, doing mobile gigs from the off, and with continuing down this avenue, I soon figured out that I needed to spread my wings and become a multi-format DJ, which is a DJ that doesn't just specialise in one genre of music (like I do now); these DJs can specialise in everything from the '60s, '70s, '80s, '90s, '00s, present, chart, club, house, disco, and whatever else you want to incorporate, really— 'not genre-specific' is a better word.

For example, when I would DJ at a wedding or birthday party, I'd have to play and be expected to play anything and everything, including multiple genres of music, in order to cater to everyone.

For YFC gigs, it was pretty much the same, but with a lot more dance/club music included.

In later years, when doing club work, I'd be playing nothing but dance music all night in one club, and then in a different club, I'd play an '80s and '90s themed night.

When doing pre-recorded DJ mixes for my Mixcloud, I play deep chilled / organic house, club classics, progressive trance, melodic trance, and funky house, which are all personal favourite genres of mine.

When doing a Dance Anthems Takeover set with Sam, I play funky house, soulful house, house, and dance classics.

So, as you can see, I'm extremely diverse in the way I play as a DJ.

There are no written wrongs and rights about what music you should specialise in at all. You play whatever you want to play and carve yourself into the DJ you want to be, but just try and figure out where you want to go, what you aim to achieve, and what you'll need to focus on. I wanted to be a DJ that could cater for any event; therefore, I chose to be a multi-format DJ, and I enjoyed being a multi-format DJ; it doesn't mean I literally play every genre of music, and there are plenty of gigs out there that I wouldn't be suited to play, but choosing this route does open up many more doors and opportunities for you, and it helps that I do enjoy a wide range of different genres of music. I've got good friends that are DJs who strictly stick to a certain genre of music that they want to play, so they may never play a wedding, a birthday, or a general club set, but they do play genre-specific events, which may mean they wouldn't necessarily be as busy as a multi-format DJ.

You'll soon find out very quickly that there are so many different genres and subgenres of music out there when you head on over to download sites to buy your music; it's important thar you don't get bogged down when you're faced with this. Focus your attention on what sounds good to you and what you like. Dance music, for example, is broken down into many sub-genres: funky house, deep house, organic house, EDM, and the list goes on and on. I couldn't believe how many subgenres there are these days, but I can assure you that, after time, patience, and familiarisation, and the more you buy your music, it will all become second nature to you. For now, call it a dance.

Your Music Collection

Now that you're figuring out what kind of DJ you want to be, you'll need a music collection. You may have already been collecting music for a long time; if so, great! This will give you a head start. If not, and you're starting a music collection from scratch, this could take a little longer, and you'll need to invest some time and money into it. For birthday and Christmas presents, I'd be asking for gift cards!

Today, however, this shouldn't take too long, as downloading is now quick and easy. There are some great places you can visit online where you can buy complete back catalogues of music, giving you a healthy, well-stocked library quickly from the comfort of your own home, which is a lot easier than getting your mate's mum to drive you miles to nose dive into a bargain bin in Woolworths. It will cost you a few quid to quickly get a healthy library if you're starting from scratch, but look at it as an investment. Once you start getting gigs, it will soon pay for itself, plus, without the music, you're not going to get a gig. Like a tradesman who buys a drill, music is your tool.

Suppose you're a specialist DJ, focussing on one style/genre of music to play. In that case, you'll be able to build a collection faster than if you're going down the multi-format DJ route; with the multi-format DJ route, if you can see yourself wanting to add weddings and birthday parties and events where you'll get a wide range of ages, you'll need all the most popular tracks ranging from the '60s right through to the present day. This may sound daunting and overwhelming, but don't let it put you off. As I mentioned above, you can buy complete back catalogues online, which are often compiled by DJs who know what you'll need and will give you all the most popular tracks from over a span of years. I personally found that one of the best ways to bulk up your collection is to invest in the Now! That's what I call music compilations. These started with Now 1 back in 1983 and are still going strong today. These are great albums for all the big hitters. I'd highly recommend a few of these in your collection. The other upside to these is that they all feature clean versions of tracks with no expletives, which will save a few head turns and dropped drinks at certain events.

There is an abundance of compilations out there, and personally, the compilations are a perfect buy and ones to have a look at to get yourself a good collection. A good place to seek out back catalogues of music and buy most genres of music is:

www.cdpool.com
www.beatport.com
iTunes
Amazon Music
www.mastermixdj.com

There are many more out there to look at, but these are the regular stops that I personally use for new music. CD Pool isn't a place just to buy a single track you want like you can on the likes of Amazon Music or iTunes; it's a pool (which I'll explain next). Beatport, however, is. You can jump on here and just buy as many or as few tracks as you like.

Once you have a full back catalogue of tracks, you could then, if you wanted, become a subscriber to a DJ pool, which is where you pay a monthly subscription to a particular package you want, and they then send you CDs and MP3 versions each month of all the latest releases, usually a few weeks or months before the tracks on them are released. These are a great way to stay up to date about new music. CD Pool, for example, is one of these; again, through a simple Google search, you'll find many pools available.

As I've explained earlier, getting a library from nothing will take some expense and time, but once you've got it, it's plain sailing from there on to keep adding to it and keeping it up to date.

If you're not a subscriber to a DJ pool, then a great way to keep up with new music and what new music is popular is to check out radio playlists. I used to religiously do this. A few days before any gig, I set aside some music 'prep' time. This time, I'd look through BBC Radio 1's top 40 charts the Dance Anthems playlist, too. This gave me a good indication of what is popular and what will ultimately be expected to be played at a gig, and it's also a great way to catch up on tracks that you may have missed by not listening to the radio. By the way, listening to the radio as much as you can is the best way to stay in the loop with commercial pop music, Radio 1 was my go-to station, and I'd listen to it whenever I could to keep my music fresh. These days, I listen to Capital Dance, which is available on DAB.

Prep time may sound boring, time-consuming, and a bit like homework, but believe me, it's vital you do it and make sure you fit in the time to do it. There's nothing worse than turning up to a gig and not having the latest tracks in your collection. You'll feel a lot more confident knowing you're all up to date with your music. Occasionally, I've missed some prep time for one reason or another, and so will you, but I always felt like I'd forgotten something when I played a gig and hadn't updated my collection. I felt a little vulnerable and on edge. To be honest, it sounds worse than it is. If you are into your music and want to be your best, you'll enjoy doing it, especially when you've got a bulk load of brilliant tracks; you'll be excited to play them. If I'm preparing for a DJ set, I almost enjoy it as much as the DJ set itself. No better feeling than knowing that you're turning up to a gig with a bag full of new bangers.

If you are totally in the dark with tracks to play or be expected to play at a wedding, for example, just jump onto Google and type in 'Top wedding songs' or something along those lines, and it won't be long before you find some cracking lists of what you'll need, what you'll be expected to play, and what you will most certainly get asked for.

So there we have it—a brief but yet essential bit of information to get started on and give you some food for thought.

Once you've got any form of music library, the most important thing you can ever do is...

Back it up!

If you're a digital DJ—and by this I mean, DJing with USB sticks, hard drives or laptops—it's absolutely paramount that you back up your music collection each and every time you add tracks or make any form of alteration; it's as simple as that. Do it the same way you'd back up a document you've been working on; you wouldn't write an essay, for example, then switch off your computer without saving it, would you? So, use the same logic when working on your music library; once you've made alterations, back it up when you're finished, and if you think you've backed it up, back it up again. Unlike CDs or vinyl, if one of those formats gets scratched, damaged, or lost, it's just one track or album that can be easily replaced. Imagine you have your whole collection of thousands of tracks on a USB stick, and it gets damaged or you lose it. I don't need to say any more. BACK IT UP! All the time, every time.

I fell victim to this once when I first started DJing with USB. Unfortunately, and stupidly, I didn't back my USB up, and it became corrupt, and guess what? I lost it all. To say I'd have much rather that a powerful, unsuspecting kick to the undercarriage is an understatement.

Luckily, though—and this was tremendously lucky—I did have a part backup from several months prior, which helped me, but I still lost approximately 100 to 200 tracks. It was awful and painstaking to recover those tracks I lost, and the only way I'd know if I'd lost that track would be when I came to play it and didn't have it, although there are easier ways now with digital DJing to see what you've lost should the worst happen (I'll cover more on digital DJing soon).

I always have my main USB stick, which I use for DJing, backed up onto a portable hard drive whenever I've finished adding tracks. This hard drive stays safely at home. I always carry an identical copy of my main USB stick to gigs with me for safety in case my main USB fails. This way, I'm comfortable knowing that all is not lost should history repeat itself.

As you can see, there's quite a lot to think about behind the scenes as a DJ that no one else sees—all of this before you even step up to the decks. For every successful DJ set, there must be some form of prep at some point behind it, and I always performed better, so you will know that some thought had gone into it.

Years back, when I first started to DJ and get gigs, I would always be up to date with my music, but with a gig ahead of me, I'd never have my music laid out to play in any particular order. In my mind, I knew the gigs I played would have some form of order. Typically, for the first hour, it would be background music, so I'd put a pre-recorded mix on. When it was time to lift the volume and get the night going, I'd be playing commercial pop music on the charts. I'd then move into a solid hour or two of pure dance tracks that were popular at the time, after that into some R&B, into some classic songs that absolutely everyone knew and would sing to, and into some 90s before finally winding it down. That is based on a typical YFC gig. That's catering for everyone pretty much and giving them a good, varied selection to keep a full dance floor. I didn't have a tracklist set out in front of me. After the experience, I just knew what tracks to play and when. This is something that you'll figure out relatively easily and that will become second nature to you.

An advantage I found to playing a mixed bag like this was that if at any time you saw the dance floor starting to thin out, you had an absolute arsenal of big hitters from all genres to pull out of the bag to keep them on the dance floor. There would be times when I'd have a packed dance floor playing dance tracks, and in my mind, I'd have several big tunes to play still. However, I noticed the dance floor getting a little tired and starting to dissipate. I'd then have to shelve the remaining dance tracks I wanted to play and either give them a miss for that gig or come back to them later. So let's say I was playing a dance track. It was starting to thin out the dance floor. My go-to track then would have been House of Pain's Jump Around. This is a massive anthem that never fails, and it kicks in immediately with a huge trumpet kind of sound that absolutely everybody recognises, which will stop them in their tracks and get them back to the dance floor pretty rapidly. With that track playing, I've instantly jumped genre to hip-hop and R&B, which changes it up and keeps them going.

It's knowing what tracks act as the glue that are key. On gigs like these and being multi-format, you can have a lot of fun and jump in and out of all genres of music to keep a full dance floor. It really can be a random and diverse gig where the sky's the limit.

If I'm doing a strictly dance DJ set, it can sometimes be a little more of a challenge than the above, as if your dance floor is starting to deplete. You really will have to know your music and think of a track that won't fail. So when doing a one-style genre of the gig, I'll always have a selection of tracks to the side that I know; if I need them, they are there and will bring the dance floor back. If I haven't needed to use them throughout my set, I'll drop them in naturally as and when. This is why it is important not to go in and start your set with all your big hitters. Pace it out and read the crowd. It's a skill that you will naturally learn, and it's the most important one. Learn how to read and steer a crowd. You can pre-prep DJ sets if you want to. I know I do on occasion where if I have a gig coming up that is in one genre, I'll make a folder or two of tracks that I will definitely play, and in that kind of order, but again, I will have a safety folder also with those go-to tracks should things get a little tricky. Personally, I'd never pre-prep a multi-format gig like a wedding or birthday; sure, I'd have a folder with all my tracks in it, but I think you'd find it quite difficult to stick to a rigorous playlist as these events differ so much. You just do not know what you'll get asked for or end up playing, which to me, was all part of the fun and kept it interesting.

DJ Software

DJ software is software you install on your laptop when using a DJ controller or for music management to export to a USB to play on CDJs.

You will need this software if you're using the above; all DJ controllers you buy will come with the software and licence ready to go straight from the box. You'll just need to download the software, enter a licence key, and register it, which takes minutes. Once registered, you'll have full access to load and play your music on your controller. This information is based on Pioneer Rekordbox DJ software, which is the software I use; other DJ software may vary on set-up. I have always used Pioneer DJ hardware and software, so I can only give you information regarding that brand. There are many other brands of DJ hardware and software on the market for you to research.

Suppose you're going to DJ purely on the Pioneer CDJ range, for example, with a USB stick. In that case, you'll still need to download the Rekordbox DJ software to organise your music library, export it to the USB stick, and then insert that directly into the CDJ.

There are a few different DJ software packages available on the market, but all in all, they do the same job; it's just your preference. If you're using the Pioneer range of controllers, you now have a choice with some, whether you use Pioneer's own software called Rekordbox DJ or Serato. Rekordbox is Pioneer's own software, which I use and think is brilliant. It's a free download and free to use; there are paid versions of it out there that unlock further features for you to use if you so wish. I have never used any other DJ software, so I'm unable to comment on it, but you'll find plenty of tutorials and reviews online to work out which may be best suited for you. Just be aware that if you're going to be using any Pioneer CDJ range of CDJs, then you'll have to have and use Rekordbox DJ for your music management; other software for DJing on Pioneer CDJs is not compatible (as of yet) if you're using USB sticks.

Virtual DJ and Serato are other popular DJ software programmes that are available on the market, but again, I've not used these and can't comment on their functionality, but reviews and tutorials are in abundance and available online to help you.

There are two modes in Rekordbox DJ: 'Export' mode, which you use when you're adding tracks and organising your library at home before a gig, and 'Performance' mode, which you switch to when you're going to DJ with it. You can use Rekordbox DJ in its export mode when plugged into CDJs instead of using USB sticks, and this is personally what I do. I link my laptop up to the CDJs using Ethernet/RJ45 leads, put Rekordbox DJ into export mode, and then this enables me to drag and drop my tracks onto the CDJs. I personally like to use this option as I like to see a big, full screen of music. Yes, it's a little extra work having to link your laptop up, but I much prefer to see a full screen of music than just a little screen on the CDJs. Again though, this is just personal preference, and I know many DJs who leave the laptop at home and are happy just to use the CDJs on their own. When using my Pioneer DDJ-1000 controller to DJ, I have to use the performance mode.

Now you are completely and utterly confused; grab a brew, take five, and then, when you're ready, let's look at the different sections of DJing... I'd get a biscuit too for this bit.

Mobile DJ

It's a commitment, hard work, and can be expensive to start with, but it all pays off in the end. Getting a complete setup from the word go is daunting, and no doubt your wallet will be burning a hole in your pocket. You may think it's impossible without a lottery win. It's not. My advice is that before you go mad and buy every piece of kit on the market, get the essential items: a pair of decks, CDJs or controllers, and some headphones. Preferably a controller, as this is an all-in-one, non-stop shop and the cheapest way to get yourself up and running.

Let me just break this down...

Decks are traditionally vinyl turntables, which is what I used to begin with and play the obvious.

CDJs are digital, multi-format playing decks; they are now the industry standard, which you will find in most nightclubs and festivals, and what the top DJs use. These decks will play CDs and MP3s. Although, as of today (2023), newer models of CDJs will no longer have the CD option on them as they are being phased out the same way car stereos did. These are superior pieces of kit, all singing and all dancing players with everything you could ever need on them, apart from a small price tag. These will set you back some serious money, but if you can afford them, you'll rest easy knowing that you can't get any better than that on the market. (Based on Pioneer's range of CDJs) Even second-hand units still hold their value well.

Controllers are great and a lot more affordable. Controllers are all-in-one units that will only play digital files such as MP3, for example. These are decks with a mixer built into them, whereas with the above CDJ, you will need to sell the family car and purchase a separate mixer. So, in essence, they are good to go straight out of the box. Some controllers have a little built-in screen on them, so you can plug in your USB stick and use the screen on them, and some require you to plug in your laptop to run them. They come with the software to install on your computer so you can manage and organise your music library. Personally, I use the **Pioneer DDJ-1000** and love it, and I use a pair of **Sennheiser HD-25** headphones. Pioneer's range of controllers is practical, portable, and easy to use (with practise).

The cost of controllers varies; you can pick them up brand new for anywhere between £250 and £1500. A good tip is to have a look at auction sites before you buy, as you can find some great bargains on these. You tend to see that people have bought a brand new controller, used it for a few months, and then realised that they either don't have time to use it or have decided that they don't want to DJ, so they sell them at a good price.

Don't feel the need to break the bank and get the most expensive controller out there. You don't need to; even the cheapest, most basic controller on the market will have everything you need to practise those fundamental skills. The more high-end expensive controllers do the same job. They've just added extras on them to enhance your DJ skills after you've mastered the basics. You don't want to run before you can walk. Saying that, though, if your budget allows, you may want to go for that next model up, as this will save you some upgrading later on.

Just think about this for a minute: you say to your friend that you have bought a controller for £250.00 and that you're going to become a DJ. Your friend then laughs at you and says that's cheap and goes on to tell you they are also becoming a DJ and have bought a controller for £1500.00; great, well done to your friend! But does that instantly make them a better DJ than you? No, no, it doesn't. That expensive controller will do the same as your £250 entry-level controller. You both need to learn the art of beat mixing before anything else. And in fact, I'll be brazen enough to say that you'll probably learn far quicker on the entry-level mixer than you would on the high-end professional one, as you'll be less distracted by all the added extras used to enhance your DJing after you've mastered beat mixing. Remember, don't run before you can walk. So don't feel the pressure to go all in to begin with. Go basic, learn the art, and master it, and yes, you can do a gig with the basic controllers.

Find somebody like Dave Cornish; by this, I mean get involved with or get to know another company that hires out equipment. This will be a massive advantage for you. Just like Dave did for me/us. These companies can fill the gaps for what you need. Of course, there will be a charge to hire, but this will be far less expensive than bankrupting yourself on a Volvo load of new gear. Also worth thinking about: if you do go all out and buy all the new gear and decide down the line that it's not what you want to do, you'll have lots of new gear that you've got to sell at a lower price than what you bought it for. If you get involved and ride around with a company like this, then not only are you gaining insight into the industry and getting all that experience, but the chances are that you may be able to hire that equipment out at a discount or, even better, for free. Do your homework; find and seek out a company that can help.

So then…

Summary

- Figure out what kind of DJ you'd like to be and what you'd enjoy.
- Get a controller, some headphones, and a pair of speakers.
- Build your music collection.
- Back up your music collection.
- Learn and master the basics.
- Get involved or get to know other DJs or companies that already do this job.
- Hire from them, learn from them, and gain some experience with them while you save or reinvest for your own equipment.

A simple Google search of any of the above equipment mentioned will take you to the right places, or tap in 'DJ Controllers', and you'll have a whole list to look at.

Get to know other DJs; a good DJ will always give make time for you and give invaluable advice and pointers at no cost to them. In this industry, your fellow DJ brothers and sisters are all in it together.

You'll find that, at some point down the line, you'll meet some DJs who don't really want to be all that helpful. That's okay; just move on and find another that will give you the time. Most will.

From the start of my DJ career, I always had someone by my side to DJ with, first with Lewis and then with Mark. I wouldn't have had it any other way; I'd much rather have someone with me when DJing, whether that be as company or someone who's DJing with me. That's just personal preference. We could never have done those large gigs if I'd gone at it alone. It would have been far too much work for a one-man band, so depending on where you see yourself with your mobile gigs, if you see yourself wanting big gigs as we did, then it would be worth considering finding someone who shares the same interest, forming a partnership, and going at it as a pair rather than solo. If you are happy to soldier on and see yourself just doing as much as you can, limiting yourself to a certain size/type of gig, and working solo doesn't phase you, then carry on.

Radio Presenter/DJ

This is a far cry from being a mobile DJ. It is a different ballgame altogether. You may be able to pick up the microphone at a gig and talk, which is great as it shows and demonstrates that you have some confidence, but believe me, this is so much different than being sat in a quiet studio room broadcasting. I'm not going to tell you all the ins and outs of radio presenting. I'll leave that to your new mentor when you find them.

Again, take the time to do some research and try to find the names of some programme controllers within a radio station. Programme controllers are the people that decide what content goes out on air on that radio station. These are good points of contact; if they can't help, they can point you in the right direction of who you need to talk to. Austin was the MD (Managing Director) of the local radio station I worked at. He was the finest example of how these MDs can be; I have been lucky, though, and all the radio MDs I've had that have hired me have been really good people and are very approachable. You'll find that smaller, local, and independent radio stations have MDs that are relatively easy to contact.

To find these, it all comes down to doing your homework and research. Find a radio station that interests you, take some time to listen to it, and get a feel for how it sounds and how the presenters present. If you do this and then manage to get some work experience there, then it won't be completely alien to you.

There's no harm in aiming high and reaching out to major radio stations; I did. I knew I was unlikely to get any response from them, but nothing ventured, nothing gained. And you're far more likely to get a response from a local radio station than you will from a major one. Remember again to walk before you run. Local radio stations are a fantastic place to learn and work; they are a small, close-knit family and will generally have much more time for you. While researching, also look into hospital radio; these are a great springboard to get some experience. Like local radio, these are in-house radio stations that broadcast only to the hospital. Like a radio station, they will have the same setup as a commercial radio station. They are generally always on the lookout for volunteers, so it's well worth looking into if you want to hit those airwaves sooner.

Be patient and polite. Radio stations are a hive of activity, and therefore you may be waiting a while for a response. You will get ignored from time to time, but don't worry about it. Just keep sending those emails and fishing, as you will get a bite one day.

If you've never broadcast before and have no experience and this is something that you want to do, personally I'd find a back route in. Don't send emails saying you want to be a presenter; politely ask if you can do some work experience at the station. If they offer you experience making cups of tea, take it! The most important thing is to get your foot through the door. Once you've got your foot through the door, this opens up all the opportunities to learn about the station, get to know all the presenters and staff there, and for them to get to know you. At this point, you can then start expressing that you'd one day like to present. Once everyone there knows you want to eventually present, you've surrounded yourself with a wealth of professional knowledge to learn, and in no time, your mentor will have you in a spare studio practising, just like Austin did for me.

As it's work experience, don't expect to get paid, and if you do get offered anything, that's a nice little bonus, but it's work experience you've asked for and voluntary work. Whatever you get offered, just grab it with both hands and run with it; the key is to get as much work experience as possible because, at the end of the day, the more you can put on your CV, the better. Sir Richard Branson of Virgin fame had a marvellous saying that went, **"If someone offers you an amazing opportunity, but you are not sure you can do it, say yes – then learn how to do it later!"** I adopted that method more than a few times.

Think about this for a minute. You may spend a lot of time at a radio station and go home each day with no money in your pocket; however, what you do have and come home with is a head full of invaluable knowledge and experience that has been given to you for free.

Club DJ

Unlike radio presenting, this avenue is very similar to mobile DJ, but with the added advantage of being so much less strenuous. With this gig, it's generally a walk-in, walk-out service. Walk in half an hour before your gig and walk out 10 minutes after your gig is finished. I'll talk more about that shortly.

When I discovered working in clubs, it was only then that I realised instantly how much easier this was.
If you land a club gig, like I've mentioned before, about walking in half an hour before your set? I only do this at the club I work at because I'm familiar with the setup and how it works. **DO NOT** do this if you're walking into a club you've never played at for the first time. The reason is simple: something will almost certainly go wrong. You'll walk into a minefield, get confused, and when you realise the clock is ticking, you'll start to panic and not think straight. This has even happened to me several times, and it's not an uncommon thing, especially if you're not the only DJ or act that performs there. It's when you get too comfortable and complacent that things will tend to catch you out.

The reason for this is that the club will have other DJs working there, and they may have the two decks and a mixer set up; however, the other DJ may choose to bring in a controller and therefore unplug some of the club's gear to set theirs up and not always put it back to how it was when they leave. Trust me; I've seen this time and time again. Not all DJs do this, but I've walked into a DJ booth before, done my set, and the next time I went back, it was all set up or not set up completely differently.

This is where I cannot stress enough to get down to the club in plenty of time, so if there have been equipment changes, you can adapt and get it to how you want it to be in good time before you start your set.

I learnt from this mistake once and was still faffing about a good 45 minutes after I was due to start my set. It's an awful experience and looks so unprofessional, not to mention stressful for you. This leads me to another invaluable piece of advice: learn how to set up your gear and learn how to set up other pieces of gear too. I don't mean to learn how the sound system is installed or how to PAT test things. I simply mean learn how your controller, for example, plugs into an external mixer. Or, how you can plug in CDJs to your controller and just learn how to plug in CDJs to a mixer and how to set up decks to a mixer in general. By learning this, you'll then, should the situation arise, be able to get everything set up as it should be. YouTube has many easy, basic tutorials on all this that are well worth watching and saving on your phone.

Here's an example: I went to the club to DJ one night. I got there a lot earlier than I usually would due to excellent taxi services that night. I was about 45 minutes early. The first thing I did when I got there was set up for the night. When I went to the DJ booth, there were no decks, just the mixer. Management went and got the decks from the other room, but they didn't set them up for me, and I wouldn't have expected them to, but my point is, make sure you know how to set this up. This wasn't an issue for me due to two really important factors: I knew what I was doing and had the time to do it. Imagine the stress and panic you'd face if you walked into the club late, didn't know the basics of setting up gear, and came across the mentioned problem.

I even have a load of notes and screenshots on my phone of certain ways to change settings that I wouldn't generally remember, so if I'm faced with changing settings one night for whatever reason, I can revert back to them. It's extremely handy and good practise to save notes and links on your phone.

The best thing you can do if you get a club gig is find out what equipment they have in the DJ booth. That would be a priority, in my eyes. You could ask to visit the venue and see the set-up they have or speak to the owner/manager prior and ask them. Better still, put it in your diary to go and visit the club one night, and then once you are there, you can go and say hello to the DJ and see what they have for yourself. Going back to doing homework, it's always good if you can visit the club you want to DJ in first, not just to have a look at the equipment, but to go there one night and get a feel for the club, see what the genre of music is, and get a general feel if it's a place you can see yourself playing in before you approach them.

The first club I worked at was comfortable. It was a club that I went to quite often when I wasn't working at weekends, so I knew what I was applying for and therefore gave myself that extra bit of comfort when I was offered a gig. If you find yourself struggling to get a response from club owners or management, don't worry; if they don't respond to you, then it might be that they don't have any vacancies, or it could be likely that they source their DJs from an agency and therefore can't offer you work as it will breach their agreement with their agency.

Agencies are a fantastic way to get into a club; these people and companies add you to their talent portfolio and get you the work. Sounds too good to be true? It really isn't. I was on an agency for a short time and would often get a call from my agent to ask if I could do X night at X club or venue. I'd then either accept or decline the gig. If I agreed, I signed a contract and was then booked for that gig. It was as simple as that. Remember, though, that if you get a job through an agency, a good bit of advice is to ask them for some details on the venue you are playing at. Your agent will let you know what the music policy is, but it's always worth asking what equipment the venue has. Most of the time, the agent will know. I always asked for my own peace of mind, and it goes back to what I was saying earlier about DJ booth setups. I always put my controller in the boot of my car, too, just in case all else failed and I didn't know what equipment I was walking into. I can only think of one occasion where this paid off: when I walked into a venue. They had two completely different sets of decks; this wasn't the worst problem in the world, and I could have continued, but it would have felt awkward to me, so the easiest thing was to get my controller plugged in.

Oh, No!

You've made a mistake, and the end of the world is nigh, right Not so much.

Every gig you will learn from, you'll have disasters, and things do go wrong! But don't worry about it; pick yourself up, dust yourself down, learn from it, and carry on. I accept, though, that sometimes that's easier said than done.

One paramount thing I did learn, and still do to this day, is that if you make a mistake, remember, you might feel like you've accidentally taken a laxative tablet instead of your multi-vitamin, but most of the time, people won't have even taken note of it. But if someone does, does it really matter? No, not at all.

If it's an obvious mistake and it's a right howler, don't get worked up over it, don't stress about it, don't take it seriously, and most importantly, don't let it ruin your gig. Have a laugh about it; take the p*** out of yourself! You'll find that people won't laugh at you; they'll laugh with you. If you're able to overcome a bad situation by not beating yourself up in front of people, you'll find it will pass quicker and easier. I once was playing a full-on club set and accidentally played 'Love Me For A Reason' by Boyzone. My CD printout didn't tally up with the tracks on the CD. I was preoccupied taking requests and didn't cue it up in my headphones before playing it.

How did it feel when I hit play? I felt like I was going into labour, if I'm honest, but the best thing I did was get on the microphone and announce something that made it more humorous, and it gave me time to find another track to play rather bloody quickly. As crazy as it may seem, it worked! Add a touch of comedy to your cock ups. If you pull a face and get all grumpy, and people see that, they'll feed off that energy, and it will make it a whole lot worse for you.

Use the Internet to your advantage

You're lucky, because, these days you can find everything you could ever want or need on the internet. There is an abundance of tutorials out there that are brilliant. I wish I had access to all this way back when I started. I still watch loads to this day; with the way DJing has evolved over the years and the more advanced decks and controllers have become, the art of beat mixing has fallen way behind. Don't get me wrong, beat mixing by ear is the foundation and is still the number one skill to learn, but the amount of effects and on-the-fly remixing and editing you can incorporate is on another level and can get a little overwhelming. But just remember the basics first, and what? Don't run before you can walk.

Below are some fantastic channels on YouTube that I subscribe to. All these have superb tutorials that are very well put together, useful and informative, and a host of good, honest advice. It is well worth checking out these channels and subscribing to them. Some of these channels also offer DJ courses on their websites too, so they could be worth looking into and something you may feel you'll benefit from. I've not done any DJ courses myself, but they do look like seriously good fun.

Phil Morse, who is the founder of **Digital DJ Tips** and is a professional DJ himself, has a fantastic book out there called 'Rock The Dance Floor; which is available to buy on Amazon; this is a brilliant read and extremely useful and informative, I can highly recommend adding it to your reading list and adding it to your journey to DJ. It's like a map is to a walker. On his YouTube channel and website, you'll find an absolute treasure trove of useful hints, tips, advice, DJ courses, gear reviews—the list goes on. He also does live Q&A sessions. **Digital DJ Tips** is an essential place to stop by.

www.digitaldjtips.com

Jamie Hartley and his team front another online DJ tutorial, a one-stop shop for everything and anything DJ, called **Crossfader**. These guys know their onions on just about everything! I highly recommend checking them out and making them essential by watching along with Phil at Digital DJ Tips. With both of these places to check out, there's no stone unturned, and they will provide you with absolutely everything you'll ever need to know, coming direct from professional DJs. **Crossfader** offers loads of advice and DJ courses too. If you check them out on YouTube, make sure you subscribe to their channels, as they do put out frequent content that you don't want to miss.

www.wearecrossfader.co.uk

Ellaskins – The DJ Tutor. Where to start with this wonderful chap. His infectious style of presentation techniques, knowledge, and professionalism will leave you nothing short of hooked. Jonathan (AKA Ellaskins) has been broadcasting and helping DJs on their journeys since YouTube started, I'd say. Jonathan is a seasoned professional DJ himself and, again, like the other guys, knows everything about DJing. He has an absolute treasure trove of brilliant videos to go through on his YouTube channel. You really are missing out if you don't head over to his place and subscribe.

www.djtutor.com

Club Ready DJ School is next up on my list of essential channels and websites to stop by. Andrew, who fronts **Club Ready DJ School,** is somewhat of a healer, in my opinion. Not only is this guy a professional DJ and tutor, but he has to be the most chilled-out man I have ever seen. His approach to his teaching is somewhat hypnotic, and you can't help but be infatuated with him. Andrew offers lots of advice and tips on his YouTube channel as well as online courses, which you can find on his website. Go check him out and kindly subscribe.

www.clubreadydjschool.com

DJ Phil Harris is last on my list, but by far not the least. Phil is another addictive character to watch. He, like the others, has a fantastic YouTube tutorial channel that guides and explains everything you need to know about DJing. I particularly like Phil's approach in some of his videos in the way he almost goes old school and becomes a teacher, bringing out the pens and the whiteboard. I like the way that he physically draws some things that are sometimes a little tricky to envisage. Phil also runs DJ courses, which can be purchased on his website. Do the right thing and pop by to give Phil some of your time.

www.beginnerdjlessons.com

If you're looking to buy your DJ gear, remember that it's well worth your time checking out auction sites first, but if you're going for something brand new or want to finance it, then be sure to have a look at these places. I've dealt with them in the past and highly recommend them; they're quick, easy, and very efficient.

www.djkit.com
www.bopdj.com

Head on over to the Bang the Stage Again! Website where you will find links to the social media pages, where I'll be posting lots of photos that relate to the stories in this book.

www.bangthestageagain.co.uk

If you're interested in listening to some of my studio mixes, you can find a selection of them on Mixcloud. These are raw, unedited mixes that I just hit record on when the mood takes me to have a mix. I don't strive to create the perfect mix; I just mix and record. Search for 'Dan Morris' or use the link below.

www.mixcloud.com/djdanmorris16940

If you want to see what myself and Sam's Dance Anthems Takeover events are all about, then take a look at our website for photos and videos.

www.danceanthemstakeover.co.uk

Facebook and Instagram search: '**Dance Anthems Takeover**'

A Controversial Myth Buster

I just wanted to put this one out there as it could sway people's thinking on digital DJing, and I wouldn't want it to put anyone off.

One thing you will see and read often during conversations and threads online is that if you're using a laptop to DJ with, then you're not a real DJ. Don't believe this. This is not true at all.

This is possibly the most controversial thing you'll see as a DJ, and it causes much debate within the community.

DJing evolved years ago, at a time when vinyl was your only option to mix. It was difficult to master the art of professional beat-mixing unless you were blessed with the gift.

CD DJing then made its way through some years later, and things started to change, making DJing that little bit easier. For one, downloading music and burning it to CD saves you the hassle of carrying around multiple heavy boxes of vinyl to each gig and creating room at the back of your car, and it is far quicker than vinyl shopping.

Moving on again, MP3s then came in with the introduction of laptops. This was another game changer; now you no longer needed to carry CDs around with you, and now your whole music collection can fit in the palm of your hand on a USB stick and into your pocket—quite a difference from a car boot full of music. With this came the skill section; you have the power of advanced software at your fingertips and equipment that would give you so much more information than a black piece of plastic would. Timings of the track, BPM, key, visual waveforms, and the list goes on. What it also gave you was a button—a button that causes the ongoing debate… sync.

The sync button, if used, will, in a nutshell, do everything for you. It will automatically snap your beat into sync the moment it is pressed or the moment you load a track. It's clever, and, when used correctly, it can save your mix if something goes wrong. I personally think it's a fantastic feature within today's digital DJing, and I don't condone anyone using it within reason. Lots of trickery DJs use it because they're so busy with everything else they are doing at a fast pace that they don't have the time to beat-match a track. The only time I ever use the sync button is, for example, if I'm mixing a tricky track and start to lose the mix. I'd much rather hit the sync button quickly, snap my beat back in, and save my mix than have a messy mix on my hands.

I think the reason people say, "You're not a real DJ" if you're using a laptop is purely for this reason. In essence, you could buy a controller today, and today, you could beat mix. It's that simple, you could. You can literally become a pop-up DJ overnight, saving you months and possibly years of mastering beat mixing by ear.

This may sound appealing, but it really isn't the best way to start. This is papering over the cracks, and if you do this, sooner or later, you'll find yourself in a predicament and receiving that sharp, swift blow, as I've mentioned before. As I've described in this book, learn from scratch, learn your music, and learn how to manually beat mix without the use of the sync button. Go right back to the basics and learn the hard way. This, I understand, may sound crazy, but why do something the hard way when there's an easy way available? The reason being, if you've started your DJ journey reliant on beat mixing using the sync button solely, what happens when you come across a time when a sync button isn't available? You may be DJing a gig on equipment that doesn't have this function, or you may turn up at a club that doesn't allow you to bring in your own controller and have to use theirs that doesn't have a sync button. I think you can see where I'm going with this—a very awkward situation. Adding to that, though the sync function is pretty clever, it's not bombproof and, from time to time, does make its own mistakes and doesn't accurately match that beat. This is when you'll have to go back to your basics and manipulate that track to get it saved. It's not much help if you're unable to beat match by ear.

Be smart, put in the hard work, and learn and master the traditional, age-old art DJ skills of beat matching/mixing. This way, you are ready and confident that you, no matter what you are faced with, will be able to beat mix successfully on any equipment in front of you. Besides, where's the fun in DJing when something else is doing it for you? The thrill in it is getting that beat matched and mixing it in, which you'll soon discover; you'll feel a sense of achievement and buzz when you do it.

With all that said, ultimately, the bottom line is…
Whether you're a vinyl DJ or digital DJ, a multi-format DJ or specialist DJ, or whatever else kind of DJ, getting a full dance floor and keeping it full by whatever means is your ultimate goal and the overall achievement you're aiming for when taking over the stage.

Just do what you do, in any form, enjoy it, and ignore any negativity surrounding this topic. I saw this quote once by the super-talented DJ and producer John Digweed, which sums it all up perfectly…

"Vinyl, CDs or laptops, it doesn't matter – you should use whatever you're comfortable with. If you're on the dance floor and there's good music coming out of the speakers, that should be enough."

And that's it—some useful advice and pointers to think about on your journey starting out as a DJ, which hopefully you'll find of some use and help.

Unfortunately, though, I'm no career advisor, and that's

probably a good thing, really, as I'm in no position to give you any career advice in alternative work, and if I did, that would definitely be of no use to you. And, let's be honest, if I were to be a career advisor and add that to the long list of my jobs, I'd have most probably quit by the time it took you to read this book.

To anyone that found this book interesting, and in the unlikely event my story has inspired you to go forth and become a DJ, whether it be on the road, radio, or club, I sincerely wish you all the success with your journey. You've just read a true-life account of what it was like for me from my own experience; hopefully, with the clangers put aside, this was enough for you to want to give it a go. Just remember to have fun and party!

Printed in Great Britain
by Amazon

27328532R00096